Stepping Out

READING AND VIEWING
Making Meaning of Text

Teacher's Resource

D1206577

PEARSON

Professional
Learning

Toronto

Library and Archives Canada Cataloguing in Publication

Kiddey, Pat
    Stepping out, reading and viewing : literacy resource / Pat Kiddey,
Richard Murray Chambers.

Co-published by: Western Australian Minister of Education and Training.
Includes bibliographical references and index.
ISBN 0-13-201857-8

    1. Workplace literacy—Study and teaching (Secondary) 2. Literacy—
Study and teaching (Secondary) I. Chambers, Richard Murray, 1948-
II. Western Australia. Minister of Education and Training III. Title.

LC149.K43 2005 Suppl. 1   428'.0071'2   C2005-904540-X

Development, Chapters 1 to 4: Pat Kiddey, Manager, Stepping Out,
Greg Robson, CEO, Edith Cowan University Resources for Learning for the Department of
Education and Training, Western Australia

The input of the following people is acknowledged and valued: Associate Professor Judith
Rivalland, Professor William Louden, and the late Ken Willis (academic staff from Edith
Cowan University, Western Australia)

Development, Chapter 5/Strategies: Pat Kiddey and Felicity Waring,
Steps Professional Development, for the Department of Education and Training, Western
Australia

Steps Professional Development is a not-for-profit organization that provides professional
development and publishes resources for teachers in the areas of literacy (K–12), mathematics,
and physical education. Steps Professional Development has offices in Australia, the United
States, and the United Kingdom and is represented in Canada by Pearson Professional
Learning.

ISBN 0-13-201857-8

Director, Pearson Professional Learning: Theresa (Terry) Nikkel
Professional Learning Manager: Marina Pyo
Canadian Edition Consultant: Rick Chambers
Project Manager: Susan Petersiel Berg
Production Coordinator: Zane Kaneps
Art Direction and Design: Alex Li
Page Layout: David Cheung
Cover Image: © Otto Steininger/Images.com
Permissions: Terri Rothman

  2 3 4 5 DPC 09 08

Stepping Out

Stepping Out was developed by Steps Professional Development on behalf of the Department of Education and Training, Western Australia.

The resource contributes to the debate about the significant number of adolescent learners who make little progress academically after their first year at secondary school, about the factors that make learning in the middle years of schooling difficult, about the culture shock of moving to a heavily subject-orientated curriculum, and about the complex nature of curriculum literacies. It supports sectors and schools as they address challenges confronting teachers during this phase of schooling.

Stepping Out focuses on improving pedagogy for all students, including those "at risk" at both ends of the academic spectrum. It provides teachers with the confidence to help all students tackle the literacy demands of learning areas. It both builds on, and extends, teachers' skills and understandings about literacy and learning. As such, it is a refresher course for those with an understanding of literacy theory, as well as a foundation course for those who have limited knowledge about literacy.

Stepping Out aligns with system mandates and initiatives. It is a conduit for developing successful whole-school and learning-area approaches that impact positively on student learning outcomes and pedagogical practices. It consists of professional development courses, learning and teaching strategies for adolescent students, curriculum support materials, and an extensive range of practical and productive approaches, processes, and strategies that assist with whole-school planning for improvement.

Stepping Out comprises three flexible modules: Writing, Reading and Viewing, and Listening and Speaking. Each module can be accessed as a stand-alone program of PD or used in conjunction with other literacy resources. The modules are available as two-day Teacher, three-day Literacy Leader, and seven-day Facilitator Training courses.

Background

Steps Professional Development was established in 1998 by Edith Cowan University to manage the redevelopment and implementation of a range of resources owned by the Department of Education and Training, Western Australia. Steps Professional Development is a wholly owned public company that is limited by guarantee and reports to the University through a Board of Directors comprised of leading educators, academics, and business representatives. The company is a not-for-profit organization dedicated to the design, development, and delivery of high-quality professional development and educational resources that enhance teacher practice and student outcomes in education communities around the world.

Suite of Resources

Pearson Education Canada manages a suite of high-quality professional development resources specifically designed to improve the learning outcomes of students in primary, middle, and secondary schools, including *First Steps* and *Stepping Out*, and *First Steps in Maths*.

The resources are all rich in educational ideas, research-based, and follow sound learning theory. Like all good ideas, however, they need to be brought to life and adapted for each context in which they are being applied. Even though they each provide clear approaches, processes, and strategies for use at the classroom, school, and sector level, they are not prescriptive band-aids or "packages" that people can follow without thinking. Participants at PD courses are encouraged to make professional judgments about what to use and when to use it. In that way, the most appropriate ideas and materials are drawn from the resources.

The following members of the Steps Professional Development team developed the Stepping Out resource for the Department of Education and Training, Western Australia:

Stepping Out Manager
Pat Kiddey

Consultants
Tania Bauk
Jacqui Hills
Maryanne Coombs
Felicity Waring
Tessa Curtis
Feni Bembridge
Robin Peters

CONTENTS

Preface

Why is it that a significant number of adolescent learners make little progress academically after their first year at secondary school? What is it about the middle years of schooling that makes learning so difficult? Is it because adolescent students have unique physical, emotional, and psychological needs and unpredictable hormones? Is it the culture shock of moving to a heavily subject-oriented curriculum? Or is it that the literacy demands of learning areas become more complex?

To understand any of the issues we must be fully aware of the context in which they exist. Each one of these factors can have a direct impact on students' learning outcomes. This text contributes to the debate and offers the best way of addressing the challenges that confront teachers during this vexing phase of schooling. It also highlights key issues and raises the awareness of teachers, school leaders, professional development consultants, and researchers about the impact on teaching, learning, and assessment.

Literacy underpins all school learning. It is the vehicle for understanding the specialized language, concepts, and skills of each learning area. When students' literacy skills are improved, they are able to process information more effectively, and they have greater understandings about subject-specific content. Their learning outcomes are therefore more likely to improve. The text provides a range of strategies that teachers can implement to address literacy across the content areas.

Teachers who are familiar with the purposes and benefits of different strategies are better equipped to cater to the diverse needs of adolescent learners. Students who can independently select and apply a range of strategies in different contexts and for different purposes are able to complete effectively the many complex tasks that they will encounter throughout their school years.

This text is a practical resource and a reference for teachers striving to cater to the learning needs of adolescent students. It is recommended that as part of this process, teachers and schools elect to engage in the Stepping Out literacy professional development program, which is designed for teachers of students aged 12 to 18 years. The program assists teachers, learning-area faculties, and whole-school staff in developing and monitoring literacy improvement across the school. All components of the program link closely to classroom practice and show how literacy strategies can be incorporated within subject-specific content in all learning areas. The program has been implemented in secondary schools worldwide and acknowledges the long-term nature of literacy improvement.

This resource emanates from the Stepping Out professional development program and may be used as a resource document (and required reading) for participants in that program.

Improving literacy skills = improving learning outcomes!

CHAPTER 1

The Middle- and Secondary-School Context

The current focus on improved student achievement is fast becoming a preoccupation in the educational community. This interest is revealed in the convergence of several developments:

- new curriculum documents
- an increased focus on adolescent learners
- an emphasis on literacy
- new accountability measures for students, teachers, and school systems

In the last several years, newly developed curriculum documents have identified hundreds of learning expectations for students in all subjects. These learning demands have been coupled with new mandates for literacy improvement across the school. The messages that accompany this shift underline the need for teachers to reflect closely on strategies and to adjust them to ensure that students meet learning expectations.

At the school level, the intensified process of accountability is encouraging many school leaders and teachers to question whether traditional school structures are assisting or hindering progress towards improved student achievement. This is particularly so in grades seven to ten. Consequently, there is a rising tide of interest in exploring alternative patterns of organizing this phase of schooling, such as grouping teachers in learning teams. These developments characterize what is termed as "middle schooling."

The emphasis on literacy is expounded at both the provincial and national levels. In the United States, state and national plans set out the accountability requirements for schools as exemplified in the No Child Left Behind legislation. In the United Kingdom, implementation of national reading strategies has raised student performance scores dramatically. In Canada, provincial governments are investing millions of dollars in developing materials to support teachers in improving students' literacy skills. All of these initiatives contain common messages about the importance of literacy as a prerequisite for making further progress through the curriculum and improving student achievement.

The convergence of all of these powerful factors has put a spotlight on middle schooling where, for many students, learning seems to stand still or even decline.

What Makes Learning Difficult in the Middle Years?

The middle years of schooling (often dubbed the forgotten, Cinderella stage of schooling) are under scrutiny in a number of countries around the world as increasing pressure is placed on government, schools, and teachers to improve student achievement. Despite the fact that many schools have implemented innovative and successful programs for students at this stage of schooling, a significant number of students continue to fall through the cracks.

Most elementary students make the transfer into senior elementary or junior high school with a minimum of fuss. They make friends easily, enjoy having a variety of teachers and a range of subject choices, and generally thrive in this new and challenging context. Others, however, don't always find it a rewarding experience.

Research shows that the majority of elementary students start their middle and secondary schooling with great enthusiasm, but by the end of their first year, many start to show a "dip" in their achievement and attitude to learning. The problem tends to compound the following year, as the same students become bored and uninspired by their schoolwork, and pre-occupied with their friendships. Their marks drop; they develop a poor image of themselves as learners and fall even further behind. They engage in negative "acting out" behaviour, neglect to hand in assignments, and start to skip classes.

> *Generally what I find in [middle and high] schools is that a very few students offer to participate … Their expressions rarely change and then only to move from boredom to condescension. . .[A]s students move through the grades, they come to value their peers more and more. Fitting in, finding a group, and forming relationships with peers become more valuable than stickers on homework papers or nods of approval from the teacher.*
> (Beers, *When Kids Can't Read*, p. 259)

Without intervention, some students' marks decline even further and the gaps in their learning widen. An anti-work peer group culture can quickly develop, without a full appreciation of the fact that working hard now will make a real difference to achievement later.

> *If reading problems continue to grow throughout the elementary school years, students reach a point where the effort they must exert to find even minimal success with reading is not worth the embarrassment they face in the process.*

For some of these dependent readers, it becomes easier to make fun of those who like to read, to treat reading with disdain, and to convince others as well as themselves, that reading "don't do nothin' for nobody." These students arrive in middle school and later in high school disengaged – from reading specifically, but often from learning in general.

(Beers, *When Kids Can't Read*, p. 260)

Unfortunately, these negative minority groups can have a large impact on the culture of the larger cohort of students (Ruddick, et al, 1996). Students whose behaviour is not usually problematic start to find schoolwork to be "boring." They become disengaged from their learning and start falling behind.

Why do many adolescent learners find it difficult to have success academically? Why do many teachers struggle to help these students learn more effectively? While it might be tempting to point to factors outside the school or to the students themselves, it is more productive strategy to identify those aspects of the school context which provide particular difficulties for students entering the middle school years.

We can begin by trying to understand what the journey from elementary school to middle or secondary school feels like for the students themselves.

The Journey from Elementary School

Elementary school students generally like school. They are accepted socially by their peers, get on well with their teachers, enjoy doing schoolwork, and view the curriculum as something that is useful and relevant (Hill, 1993, p 14). They enjoy being at the top of the "pecking order" in their last year of school, and relish the extra responsibilities and privileges that this brings.

When the same students arrive at the middle or secondary school, they immediately become the youngest, most inexperienced, and most powerless of the school population. The culture shock they experience during this transition process can be similar to the culture shock experienced when moving from Hawaii to Bosnia (Hargreaves, 1998). They have to adjust to a larger campus, new surroundings, a more impersonal culture, a diverse curriculum, new ways of learning, and a different organizational structure. The differences between the primary and secondary contexts are stark, even though students from both sectors are chronologically similar.

Perhaps the most important differences students have to face in relation to their learning are to do with three issues:

• school organization (time, curriculum, and structures)

• approaches to teaching and learning

• increased literacy demands

Interestingly these three issues are also the issues that many teachers identify as ones they would like to address in order to help students learn more effectively.

School Organization

Structures Traditional secondary school classes and timetables tend to be organized in much the same way that they were organized 20 or 30 years ago, despite the fact that they now cater to a very different generation of students and in a climate of more intense scrutiny.

> With increased accountability, American schools and the people who work in them are being asked to do something new – to engage in systematic, continuous improvement in the quality of the educational experience of students and to subject themselves to the discipline of measuring their success by the metric of students' academic performance. … Schools, as organizations, aren't designed as places where people are expected to engage in sustained improvement of their practice, where they are supported in this improvement, or where they are expected to subject their practice to the scrutiny of peers or the discipline of evaluations based on student achievement.
>
> (Elmore, *Bridging the Gap Between Standards and Achievement*, 2002, pp. 2-3)

Of course, organizational structures do not automatically determine what happens in a school. People do. But organizational structures do influence the culture significantly. The challenge for schools is to analyze critically the impact of their own organizational structures on students' learning. The degree to which the school culture is affected by the organizational structure of the school will differ from context to context. In an analysis of secondary schooling, Fullan and Hargreaves (1991) describe the contrasting cultures that can emerge as a result of different organizational structures.

At one end of the continuum the culture can be characterized as "fragmented individualism," as represented in the following diagram:

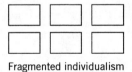

Fragmented individualism

Teachers in this type of culture tend to work alone in their classrooms, in professional isolation. They construct learning programs and evaluate their success as separate, stand-alone "units of delivery." The only meaningful feedback they receive about the effectiveness of their teaching comes from their own observations of the students they teach.

This means that there is a ceiling limit on the effectiveness and innovation of their teaching practice, which is confined to their own experiences, their own interpretations, and their own motivation to seek improvement. Inevitably, this type of organizational structure results in a narrower range of teaching practices.

Further along the continuum, Fullan and Hargreaves describe what they term as a "balkanized culture," represented in the following diagram. In this environment, departments or faculties tend to operate as separate, sometimes competing groups within the school. This reduces teachers' collective capacities, restricts opportunities for them to share their knowledge and experiences, and reduces openness, trust, and support between teachers from different subject departments.

In this type of organization, there is potential for teachers to have inconsistent expectations for students' performance across the school, and for there to be poor continuity in monitoring students' progress.

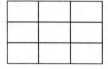

Balkanized groups

By contrast, and at a further point along the cultural continuum, there is the "collaborative" secondary school culture. Teachers in this environment recognize that teaching is difficult, and that giving and receiving help does not imply incompetence. They flesh out issues together in order to reach agreement, and seek continuous improvement in their teaching. They examine their existing practices critically, continuously test and modify their programs, seek better alternatives, and work hard to bring about improvement, both in their teaching and in students' learning.

This type of collaborative culture tends to be more receptive to change.

Collaborative culture

"Imagine that you can become a better teacher, just by virtue of being on the staff of a particular school; - just for that one fact alone."
(Little, 1990, cited in Fullan and Hargreaves (1991, p. 46))

Time In elementary schools, students reap the benefits of learning in a smaller, nurturing environment with one teacher, and with one group of students. Flexible time allocations in the elementary school make it possible for teachers to incorporate innovative methods of teaching and to plan a multidisciplinary or integrated curriculum. Teachers can more easily identify students' emotional and learning needs because they can routinely observe students working in a range of different contexts over longer periods of time. There are plenty of opportunities for students to talk and work collaboratively with others, because the majority of primary classrooms are set up to facilitate small-group learning.

Time is organized differently in secondary schools. The large number of students and the need to match specialist teachers to class groupings cause secondary schools to place the timetable at the forefront of their planning and organization. Timetabling constraints can place severe limits on innovative teaching practice. By the time the class has settled, latecomers have been accommodated, the attendance has been taken, and links have been made to the last lesson, a considerable amount of teaching/learning time has already been absorbed.

Block schedules, semestered timetables, 75-minute classes, whole-year programs with 45- or 50-minute periods, split classes, special events, and extended holidays often make it difficult for teachers to retain continuity and for students to stay focused. Timetables and time constraints can limit a teacher's ability to develop effective working relationships with students, to implement integrated learning programs, to team-teach with peers, to work collaboratively with other teachers, and for students to spend the time that is required to work through processes that lead to better learning.

Integrated Curriculum Curriculum — prescribed by provincial guidelines and moderated by local initiatives — identifies what students should be able to know and do. Teachers set out to help students realize the expectations of the curriculum. Students, on the other hand, may not necessarily be motivated to learn the content as described in the curriculum, and they may not have the skills to enable them to learn it. The range of literacy skills that students need in order to read, view, write, and interact effectively with technology to absorb the curriculum content cannot be considered "givens" when students enter middle and secondary schools.

In many secondary contexts, students are exposed to a curriculum divided into discrete units or subject areas taught by a variety of specialist teachers. This structure usually means that teachers with expertise in a particular area work apart from those in other areas, teaching in separate classrooms and often unaware of what is being taught in other parts of the school or across different learning areas.

Timetables, teaching workload, lesson preparations, pupil-teacher contacts, extra-curricular responsibilities, supervision and other factors can limit teachers' time to interact with each other on the job. There is often little time to share teaching experiences, plan cross-curricular or interdisciplinary units, share skills and expertise, moderate their judgments about students' achievement on common assessment tasks, or analyze issues related to individual and groups of students.

As a result, teachers don't often get the chance to help students to see links among topics, establish wider views of issues, or enrich their understandings and skills across the school's content areas. Learning can become fragmented as students pick up small chunks of information from each particular subject area but are not invited to see the connections among the subjects.

This means that students are learning a little bit about a lot of different subject areas – it is a curriculum that promotes memory work and rote learning, emphasizing coverage rather than understanding.

(Leithwood and McAdie, "Less Is More: The Ontario Curriculum That We Need", *Orbit*, Vol. 35, no. 1, 2005, p. 8)

Even if the learning experiences themselves are extremely effective, it is difficult for students to make meaningful connections across subject areas if the links are not identified for them. When students experience disconnected and fragmented learning on a daily, weekly, or yearly basis, they are left to link common threads among subjects by themselves. Unfortunately, not all are able to do this.

> *This kind of curriculum is not the most efficient or most effective means for developing basic skills, and it actually stands in the way of developing the more complex outcomes we aspire to for our children. A more lasting and equitable approach would ensure that all students are encouraged to be critical thinkers, to develop skills that go beyond the specific curriculum. . . [W]e need a quite different alternative, one that values and promotes deep understanding as the overarching goal for public education in the province.*
>
> (Leithwood and McArdie, p. 8 , 2005)

Approaches to Teaching and Learning

Curriculum organization flows over into teaching and learning practices. In the middle years, the curriculum shifts from being generalized and integrated to being structured and specific. It also becomes more concept- than content-based. Tight timelines to "cover" the content can result in teacher-centred lessons where buckets of information are poured into student receptacles.

As a result, adolescent learners often become flooded with facts and have to scurry through copious amounts of subject-specific content. Middle and secondary school teachers, faced with an array of classroom groupings, challenging behaviours, and demands for course coverage, can easily be tempted to play it safe by restricting the pedagogy, narrowing the curriculum design, and limiting the degree of interaction.

> *Too many students say they are just "hanging in" until Grade 12 to get their diploma. Those who do hang on until they graduate often feel alienated from learning and vow that they will not set foot in a school again.*
>
> *The problem is the curriculum. The curriculum of Canada's high schools has become bloated, fragmented, mired in trivia, and short on ideas. It does not demand that students connect what they learn with anything else or challenge them to reach beyond their limits. The curriculum stifles curiosity. Although it demands effort, it does not reward deep thought.*
>
> (Ungerleider, "The Challenge of Secondary Curriculum Reform," *Orbit*, vol. 35, no. 1, 2005)

Teachers face multi-faceted dilemmas of helping students to learn, ensuring that mandated curriculum is delivered, of establishing student-centred learning environments in their classrooms, of meeting the needs of the range of learners before them, and of balancing personal and professional responsibilities.

When asked what they expected from good teachers, secondary school students in a Kitchener, Ontario study said that good teachers:

• model the behaviour that they want from their students – punctuality, respect, discipline, hard work, good writing, a reading habit

- encourage students to work with, and to learn from each other
- learn with their students; there is no necessity to be the "fountain of knowledge"; students like to know that teachers don't know everything – it makes them more human
- encourage students to think for themselves, to be critical thinkers, to be creative and lateral problem solvers
- create an environment in which learning can comfortably take place
- allow students to construct their own meaning; let them make the work their own, not the teacher's interpretation alone
- allow students time to work; don't interrupt
- encourage students to take responsibility for their own learning; give away responsibility; help students grow; negotiate consequences beforehand; be positive
- differentiate between teaching and learning: a teacher's job should be to encourage learning, and to focus on how to help students learn
- provide opportunities for demonstrations of learning, other than testing
- avoid asking students to memorize useless information
- validate students' ideas: allow them to be creative; allow them to make mistakes; encourage their learning through risk-taking and experimentation
- use an action research approach to learning which emphasizes students' reflection on their learning
- make reflection a part of their curriculum: give students time to reflect on how and what they're learning
- use rubrics when they evaluate; negotiate rubrics with classes
- set clear expectations for a class or an assignment
- be patient, unbiased, open minded; set high but realistic standards; make learning fun
- remember what it was like to be a student.

(Strickland, Kathleen and James. *Reflections on Assessment*. Portsmouth, New Hampshire: Boynton/Cook, 1998, pp. 176-178)

As Kylene Beers asks (p. 259), what happens to that first-grade enthusiasm for school by the time students reach the middle and secondary years? For adolescent learners, the first flush of enthusiasm and any successful learning experiences can seem to have happened a long while ago — and the finishing line for the schooling journey still seems a long way ahead.

Content versus Process

Teachers often share their students' perceptions. Many middle- and secondary-school teachers comment that there is too much content to deliver and too little time to do it. A curriculum that is a mile wide and an inch deep perpetuates the idea that breadth, and not depth, is the goal of education.

Content is important but it is just as important to remember that much of what is taught today might be irrelevant or obsolete in a few years' time. Students complain that they spend far too much time learning about things that they don't believe will ever be useful to them. What really matters, and what is important, is that they are equipped with transportable tools for learning that they can apply to any body of content — in other words, learning how to learn.

There are many things that we might do to create a more challenging and meaningful school curriculum. We can do it by getting clear about what we are trying to achieve and sharpening our thinking about how the goals might best be achieved.

Getting clear on what's important for young people. . .
1. *a strong foundation in reading, writing and numeracy*
2. *being disposed to treat others with respect*
3. *having the ability to work cooperatively with others*
4. *being able to appreciate and act upon the values and principles that make us human*
5. *having an understanding of Canada and being able to appraise its strengths and limitations*
6. *being able to exercise a critical intelligence that is adaptable to circumstances unforeseen.*

(Ungerleider, p. 4)

Simply "covering" or teaching a topic does not guarantee that learning has occurred. Students learn best when they are given time to express and absorb or internalize the information. They need time to listen, read, think, talk, plan, write, and reflect on and represent their understandings. They need to do these things independently and with others. Once they have internalized the information, they can apply or translate it to other contexts.

Assessment

As students make the transition from elementary school to middle or secondary school, the stark differences experienced in curriculum organization and pedagogy carry over into the assessment practices they face. Part of the transition experience is an increase in the seriousness with which the community regards the business of schooling. The process of sifting and sorting students for further phases of education and for life beyond schools starts in earnest in the middle-school years.

As a consequence, the assessment policies and practices of most middle and secondary schools, and the formality and weight put on the reliability of assessments, reflect this increase in seriousness.

Adolescent learners are faced with a diet of frequent, content-focused testing within each subject area, the advent of formal exams in secondary schools, and a much stronger emphasis on formal expository writing. The purpose of the assessment process shifts to a preoccupation with the allocation of grades or levels. This information often starts to count towards the external purpose of assessment: to meet requirements for access to subjects in secondary school or post-secondary destinations. There is much more of a feeling in the middle and secondary context that assessment is something that is "done" to students. All too often the compromise is weighted toward responding to the external pressures, at the expense of the needs of adolescent learners.

Some of the features of assessment in the middle years are:

Over-assessment There is a tendency to over-assess students in middle school and lower secondary school to cope with the increasing demands of the curriculum and to supply information for accountability purposes.

Narrowness While there is a lot of assessment going on, much of it is narrow in focus and is concentrated on measuring whether students have acquired course content.

Lack of integration Much of the assessment is summative and can be regarded as being tacked on to learning and teaching, rather than being an integral part of it.

Student numbers and specialization Teachers in primary schools get to know their students well and are able to collect rich diagnostic information. The sheer weight of student numbers that secondary teachers have responsibility for, and the limited time they see them, makes the use of devices such as developmental continuums problematic. Middle and secondary teachers feel snowed under when they are given a large amount of information that they cannot use effectively.

Increasing Literacy Demands

Perhaps the biggest single challenge adolescent learners face is the sharp increase in demands on their literacy skills. The first year of secondary school is probably the most difficult, because of the

- increased amount of reading in all subject areas
- increased difficulty in level of concepts in all readings
- variations in teaching methods which each new subject teacher presents
- large class sizes which make individual assistance difficult either before or after lessons
- peer pressure, which prohibits being identified as needing assistance, let alone accepting any prolonged help

Literacy is not one thing evenly spread across the curriculum. It looks different and takes on different forms in different subjects and classrooms (Kress, 1999). Each learning area has its own curriculum literacies (subject specific terminology, concepts, skills, and understandings) and ways of viewing the world to understand. There are some similarities in what students might do by way of writing, reading, listening, and speaking in each subject area, but the results tend to be different, because each subject uses its own language, conventions, and structures. A procedure written in a science or physical education lesson, for example, will not look the same as a procedure written in an English lesson. There may be similarities in the form of the writing, but the terminology, tone, and content of the procedure will differ. Students have to learn to adapt to the varying literacy demands of different areas and to master these variations.

Curriculum Literacies

All learning areas place literacy demands on students. A "literacy demand" refers to any task that requires students to use literacy skills to demonstrate skills and/or understandings.

Those who struggle to meet the literacy demands of different subject areas are likely to have difficulty adequately demonstrating effective learning outcomes. In every lesson, students face a wide range of challenging literacy demands. For example, students have to be able to recognize, understand, and use the specialized vocabulary of each subject.

peninsula   vaporization   sparingly soluble   theme
SYMBOL   PASCAL PROGRAMS   monarchy
hypothesis   metaphor   RATINGS
ecosystem   rotational symmetry   friction   theology
RATIO   measure of central tendency   mitosis   apparatus
NUTRITION   plate separation   protein-rich
precipitation   point of view   principles of movement   protons
COMMERCIAL   Canada's Food Guide   neural
dependent variable   spreadsheet   neurons
proletariat   input, processing, and output   Agrarian revolution   scientific method
climate region   balanced diet   dictatorial powers
statute law
character   minor analgesics   caricature
plot   large capacity   conclusion

The literacy demands of each learning area can differ in both subtle and overt ways, and they increase in complexity and difficulty as students move through their schooling.

Grade 9	Grade 10	Grade 11
impact	satellite	nuclear fusion
comet fragments	sun synchronous	neutron star
accurate	geosynchronous	absolute magnitude
nebulae	infrared light	photosphere
black holes	remote sensing	chromosphere
quasars	maria	plagues
pulsars	microgravity	prominences
perigee	vaporizing	emission spectrum
waning	power	solar stills
solar eclipse	gravitational force	photovoltaic cell
kuiper belt	cosmonauts	interstellar
neap tide		spicules

Students have to be able to read, make meaning of, locate, and extract important information embedded in different genres and in subject-specific texts:

Inertia also works on moving bodies. A body in motion will keep moving at the same speed and in the same direction (uniform motion) unless some outside force is exerted on it and causes some change. The moving body's inertia is its property of resisting my attempt to change its motion.

PQRST is a square-based pyramid with a base of side length 14mm, and height of 6mm. The point x is vertically below T on the base, and point y is midway along PQ.

I collapsed in the armchair in a fit of despair. I had no way of knowing if my thoughts and feelings had actually reached her in some way and motivated her phone call, or if she had simply followed some intuition of her own.

The climates of Europe are dominated by the westerlies. These are on-shore winds that blow from the Atlantic Ocean. They are associated with rain-bearing depressions (low pressure areas) called mid-latitude lows. Mid-latitude lows produce the cool, cloudy and damp weather so common in northwestern Europe.

Rare earth metals (lanthanides) are used to make very powerful super magnets. Ferrite used in ordinary magnesium (a rare earth) can make a super magnet. In medicine, super magnets are used in extremely sensitive probes that provide scans inside the human body.

They must internalize and then transform information into a variety of written or oral forms that demonstrate their understanding.

The water in a mountain stream is usually crystal clear. After heavy rain, however, the stream would become muddy. Explain in your own words, why this is so.

Describe what happened to the mothballs. Draw a picture to illustrate your observations.

What is the difference between speed and velocity?

Footprints left in sand on Earth's surface last a very short time. Why should footprints on the moon last for thousands of years?

Define the word "drug." Explain why tobacco and alcohol are drugs.

What are the major uses of uranium? Why is the mining of uranium so controversial?

Students must also become adept at
- reading and writing multimedia texts
- using different learning technologies
- critically analyzing and interpreting new types of texts in different ways
- understanding how texts explicitly and implicitly influence them

Multiplicity of Demands

Recent research (Wyatt-Smith & Cumming, 1999) suggests that teachers can often be unaware of the literacy demands they place on students. In the middle years of schooling, students spend less time explicitly learning literacy skills because it is assumed that they have accumulated the skills that are required to tackle more complex literacy demands. The literacy demands of different learning areas increase as students move up through school, and students are expected to tackle not one literacy demand at a time, but a range of writing, speaking, listening, interpreting, and critical thinking demands simultaneously.

One student, observed in a science classroom during a study,

> "... was interpreting a stream of rapid verbal English from his teacher, and the writing and layout information on an overhead transparency. He was writing layout diagrams, symbolic notations, and mathematics in his personal notebook; observing the teacher's gestures, blackboard diagrams and writing; observing the actions and speech of other students, including their manipulation of demonstration apparatus, and the running commentary of his next-seat neighbour. In fact, he quite often had to integrate and co-ordinate most of these either simultaneously or within a span of a few minutes. There is no way he could have kept up with the content development and conceptual flow of these lessons without integrating at least a few of these different literacy modes almost constantly."
>
> (Lemke, 1999, p. 23)

These types of demands are compounded for many students, because in some subject areas:

> "many of the words are new or unfamiliar, the meanings being made are about strange matters of which he or she has no personal experience, the diagrams and graphs and formulas may bear only an outline resemblance to any seen before, the problems are difficult for his or her current level of mastery, the subject matter is abstract, and the problems of mutual co- ordination and calibration of all of these channels and literacies and activities are very substantial indeed."
>
> (Lemke, 1999, p. 23)

This scenario is acted out, not just in one classroom, but also in a range of classrooms, every hour, every day, and every week. In every lesson, students face a wide range of challenging literacy demands. The degree to which they master these demands impacts on their academic success.

Students who struggle to meet the literacy demands of different subject areas are likely to have difficulty adequately demonstrating effective learning outcomes. This is because attaining competence in a subject area means attaining competence in being able to read, write, and talk about it. This is what is meant by the term "literacy."

Improving the Situation

What might reduce the difficulties that so many adolescent learners experience in the middle years of schooling?

Outside school factors are certainly an influence — home environment, socioeconomic status, language, physical and emotional health, rapid changes in technology, and many other considerations.

Research on student achievement, however, points unfailingly in one direction when talking about the most significant factor in improving student performance. Far and away the single most important influence on a student's success is the quality of the teaching to which that student is exposed.

Lawrence Ingvarson from the Australian Council for Educational Research in an unpublished paper for the Australian College of Educators said that what teachers know and do is the most important influence on what students learn (2002). Even given the variations from classroom to classroom and school to school, any variations in what students actually learn is directly attributable to what their teachers know.

By the late 1990s, Dr. Linda Darling-Hammond in the United States had clearly demonstrated the importance of teacher quality in determining student success. In a report in 1997, she said that "what teachers know and can do is crucial to what students learn" (p. 1).

> *Furthermore, studies discover again and again that teacher expertise is the most important factor in determining student achievement, followed by the smaller but consistently positive influences of small schools and small class sizes. That is, teachers who know a lot about teaching and learning and who work in environments that allow them to know students well are the critical elements of successful learning.*
>
> (Darling-Hammond, p. 2)

Darling-Hammond also talks about the importance of investing in good teachers and the consequences of settling for poor or mediocre teaching. Teachers' professional knowledge, skill in helping students to learn, instructional strategies, classroom management, and interpretation of students' written and oral work are fundamental in assisting students to achieve. "Nothing can fully compensate for the weakness of a teacher who lacks the knowledge and skill needed to help students master the curriculum" (p. 2).

In fact, a Tennessee study conducted in the late 1990s found that elementary school students who were unlucky enough to have poorly performing teachers for three years in a row scored 50 percentile points lower on achievement tests than students who had more effective teachers over the same period of time (p. 6).

Effective teaching includes knowledge of the subject matter, professional knowledge about how students learn and develop, and a continually increasing repertoire of teaching and learning strategies. The myths about "anyone can teach" and "teachers are born and not made" are simply not true. There is no doubt that an individual takes a particular attitude to the work of being a teacher. A teacher's disposition — behaviour, motivation, aspirations, commitment — to work with children is undeniably an important factor in the success of an effective teacher. Equally important, however, is the training that the teacher takes to the job. There are skills, techniques, strategies, moves, content, facts, information, and insights that well prepared, formally educated teachers take to the classroom that will enable students to grow intellectually and succeed academically.

The evidence shows that students of fully qualified, dedicated teachers achieve at higher levels than those with less well prepared teachers.

In the middle school years, effective teaching requires flexible approaches, alternative courses of action, and wherever possible, whole-school strategies to address the needs of the learners. Most importantly, teachers need opportunities to talk about their students so that they can learn from each other and share understandings about

- the unique needs of adolescent learners
- factors that have an impact on students' learning in middle and secondary schools
- literacy demands that students encounter across different subject areas
- principles that underpin adolescent learning
- effective strategies to maximize students' achievement

CHAPTER 2 Adolescent Learners

Between Childhood and Maturity

Adolescents between the ages of 10 and 16 are adjusting to profound physical, social, and emotional changes. During this period they are beginning to develop a strong sense of their own identity and learning how to establish personal and working relationships with adults. They are also beginning to establish their own sexual identity. They can be passionate and egocentric about issues that they believe in, and their behaviour can be erratic, fluctuating from being cynical, sullen, withdrawn, and resistant one minute, to fun-filled and gregarious the next. During adolescence, students start to accept responsibility for making their own decisions. While they are growing towards independence, many of them are still not able to be self-regulating (Eyers et al. 1992).

Why Adolescent Learners Are Different

Adolescent learners no longer think like younger children. They are conceptually more sophisticated as learners and are able to think in ways that become progressively more abstract and reflective. They are starting to show concern about wider contemporary issues and are trying to make sense of the social and political world beyond their own communities, especially in terms of how if affects them. As learners, they are at once listless and energetic, curious and bored, maddeningly obtuse and refreshingly insightful. They are keen to get "out there" in the real world and want to learn in different contexts and in different ways.

Adolescent learners are going through a rapid growth and extensive maturation phase and are not yet independent. They are learning to understand themselves. Their learning outcomes can be greatly affected by their physical, social and emotional needs, and these must be addressed directly in teaching and learning programs.

Adolescents will often challenge authority and strongly test the boundaries of adult conventions, practices, and values. At this stage of their development, they are trying to establish new relationships when their life is characterized by storm, crisis, and harmony. They are likely to run into different sets of relationship issues as they test boundaries and question authority. If there is to be any conflict that strains family relationships, this is the time when it is most likely to occur. The conflict is not necessarily restricted to parents — it may occur with other authority figures such as teachers, police, and sports coaches.

Adolescents are passionate about the things they are interested in, and they have a tendency to become preoccupied with fashion, popular culture, and electronic and on-line games. For many, life outside school, which incorporates their interests in pop and media culture, digital learning technologies, music and fashion, is infinitely more exciting than life at school. They leave these interests outside when they enter school and therefore learning tends to be something that is disconnected from their personal experience.

Whereas teachers may be hesitant about using digital learning technologies, adolescents are largely at ease experimenting with and manipulating these tools. This may seem to be just a surface interest, but adolescent learners often demonstrate a remarkable capacity to be innovative. They also appear to be fearless about experimenting with the latest technology. It is easy to dismiss their fascination with computer games, popular culture, and fashion as superficial, or as part of an attachment to the latest fad. It is, however, often the challenge of mastering "new forms" or a new "game" that provides a motivating factor for learning. Adolescent learners respond positively to meeting these types of challenges.

Adolescent learners' self-image is greatly influenced by their level of acceptance within their peer group. Their attachment to peers is extremely powerful, and many are part of the sub-culture of groups and gangs. They afford their schools and their teachers much less importance and respect. While they seem to disguise it from time to time, they seek acceptance from adults and consequently, as learners, they prefer to be able to negotiate their learning with their teachers, through extension work, independent study, research investigations, open investigations, and group research.

This particular generation of students is being prepared for an uncertain future, and for jobs that have yet to be invented. The diversity of social contexts within which they are located and the challenges they face today are far greater than those faced by earlier generations of students. They face changes in family structures, in the types of employment that they can access, and rapid changes in learning technologies. Even the nature of learning has become more complex. The challenge is to empower them to become effective, independent learners through self-directed and self-managed learning.

Education is life — not a preparation for life. Adolescents should be viewed as real human beings that have serious questions and concerns. Their dignity must be respected.

(Beane, 1990, p. 49)

Studies of adolescent learners in Australian schools (PNS 1996, Hill 1993) reveal that students want to be engaged in interactive and collaborative approaches to their work. They want their teachers to use student-centred teaching, learning, and assessment practices, and a broader range of teaching styles and strategies than traditional teacher talk, note-taking exercises from the board, handouts, and questions and answer exercises. They enjoy being actively involved in all learning tasks and feel they need opportunities to take on work within and beyond their school context. In other words, they want to be:

"active resources for learning, rather than passive recipients of knowledge. They believe that their knowledge, views and concerns about educational and social issues are not always recognised as being a valuable curriculum resource, and that they bring a range of diverse skills that can contribute to the learning process — as researchers, producers, peer tutors, junior sports coaches, etc."

(Cumming, 1994)

General Learning Principles

The characteristics of adolescent learners are not always addressed in the middle and secondary school context. Powerful learning principles can also be ignored or overlooked at this phase of schooling. Many sets of principles that facilitate learning have been offered to teachers in the past. *Stepping Out* draws heavily from the statement below, which has a strong emphasis on purposeful and focused learning while also elegantly summarizing contemporary understandings about effective learning.

A supportive learning environment where students feel valued and challenged, and where they are able to experiment safely and work collaboratively with others.

Opportunities to learn where students encounter and are engaged by their learning, and where they have opportunities to observe, practice, develop, and apply new skills and understandings.

Connection and challenge where learning links to students' existing knowledge and skills and stretches them beyond what they know and can do.

Action and reflection where students experience learning as an active process and use language as a tool for learning. They also get opportunities to reflect on and make sense of the action.

Motivation and purpose where learning experiences are focused on achieving clear, relevant outcomes that make sense to students.

Inclusivity and difference where students engage with experiences that respect and reflect differences between learners.

Independence and collaboration where students work together (as well as individually) to ensure a personal grasp of concepts.

Curriculum Framework, W.A., 1998

Principles for Adolescent Learners

The general learning principles described apply to students from the early years to the post-compulsory years of schooling. They are clearly important. However, because adolescent learners have their own unique needs, they require a focus that applies specifically to them.

Stepping Out has a set of principles that it calls the 5 Ms. The 5 Ms reflect the things that really count, and if the aim is to improve learning in the middle years, then they need to be taken seriously.

Making Them Feel Safe

Adolescent learners learn more effectively when they learn in a safe environment and when they know that others like and value them. Teachers have a huge influence on students' self-esteem. Their perceptions, expectations, and interactions can make a real difference to learning outcomes.

Making Connections

Learning is enhanced when connections are made to

- developmental levels
- existing skills, knowledge, and experiences
- family, language, cultural, and socio-economic experiences
- individual learning styles
- peers in the classroom
- learning in primary school
- learning in other subject areas
- school community members

Making Learning Meaningful

Subject-specific content is better learned through exciting and motivating processes where learning is contextualized, relevant, and challenging.

Moving Them Forward

All students need support to make progress with their learning. They require different support (scaffolding) at different stages of their learning to enable them to achieve their target outcomes.

Making Sure They're Learning

It is important to know where students are in relation to learning outcomes, to ensure that current teaching and learning practices provide opportunities for students to achieve outcomes. Students' progress should be monitored by collecting information about processes, products, and performances over a period of time and in a range of different contexts. If students are not making progress, then something needs to change.

Making Them Feel Safe

Teachers' Interactions and Expectations

Adolescent learners learn more effectively when they learn in a safe environment and when they know that others like and value them. Teachers have a huge influence on students' self-esteem. Their perceptions, expectations and interactions can make a real difference to learning outcomes.

Students always remember the teachers who made them feel that they were a valuable member of the class.

> *"Good teachers are those you can talk to — who are understanding and show respect for people with different ideas…who are interested in us as individuals."*
> (Student, SA field study, 1994)

Research has demonstrated consistently that teachers' expectations, attitudes, and opinions have a significant influence on students' success at school. This phenomenon, called the "self-fulfilling prophecy," (Rosenthal, 1968) suggests that students become "what they are expected to become." When teachers believe that particular students can't achieve, those students' performance can be influenced in negative ways. When teachers believe that particular students can achieve, they tend to

- interact and react warmly with them
- provide more feedback about their performance
- encourage their efforts more
- teach them more difficult material
- give them more opportunities to respond and question

Students work harder for teachers who notice their efforts. They will (quite happily) provide work of a higher standard for the teacher who expects it, and work of a much lower standard for the teacher who does not expect it. It can be an interesting exercise to compare the work of one or two "target" students as they work in different classes with teachers from various subject areas. Some students' work will differ enormously from class to class. As a result of this type of analysis, some schools have negotiated a "minimum standards" requirement across the school. When high standards are expected, and explicit and ongoing and encouraging feedback is provided, students feel that the extra effort they have put into their work has been noticed and valued. This makes them feel good about themselves.

The Learning Environment

In the rush to cover course content and to fit into the tightly organized pattern of operating in a middle or secondary school, it is easy to overlook the importance of a supportive learning environment. During adolescence, however, students start to question the values, beliefs, practices, and conventions that they come in contact with. This is expected behaviour for this age group, but it can sometimes create conflict.

Adolescent learners need opportunities to express themselves in a "safe" place, free from harassment, sarcasm and remarks that denigrate their input. They need to be able to try a wide range of things, secure in the knowledge that while errors might be painful, they can often impart a lesson. They need to work with people who let them know that they are liked and trusted and that their input is valued. They also need to work in an environment that is conducive to forming relationships with teachers and peers — one that helps them move safely through this particular phase of their development.

A child's life is like a piece of paper, on which every passer-by leaves a mark.
(Chinese proverb)

Making Connections

Learning programs for adolescents require teachers to connect to, and challenge, what students already know and can do. This involves connecting to, recruiting, building on, and expanding what students know. These processes are critical elements of any learning program, and need to be made at a variety of levels.

Connecting to Developmental Levels

The implications for developmental learning theory are that teachers need to know the stage of development of their students so that they can put in place appropriate learning strategies and activities to help students progress towards the next stage of development.

In elementary schools, different levels of achievement between students can be expected. By middle school, these differences can also be expected, but are often magnified and accentuated when a number of primary school students arrive on the one site. Gaps in ability tend to widen as students move through their schooling. Those who have mastered the basic tools of learning can apply them to learn new concepts as the curriculum becomes more demanding, but those who are still struggling to come to grips with the basic skills face the prospect of falling further behind their peers. Barber (1999) suggests that a "significant number of 'lost boys,' who fail to learn to read and write well by age eleven, will never recover educationally."

What seem like small differences in achievement in the early years can be accentuated when students reach the secondary context. The developmental diversity of this age group makes it difficult to organize an educational program that adequately meets the needs of all. Compared to the breakthroughs and developmental leaps associated with early learners, progress in achievement tends to be more subtle in the adolescent years. It is therefore more difficult in the middle years of schooling to observe whether students are making progress. Consequently, we find an increasing array of labels (such as specific learning difficulties, A.D.D, dyslexia, cultural, gendered, and socio-economic groups) are used to try to explain why some students find it difficult to learn in the middle years of schooling.

Adolescent learners develop and learn in different ways. What they learn, how they learn, the rate at which they learn, and the order in which they learn are shaped by the social contexts within which they interact. Typically, they go through different stages as they develop in an area of learning, and the characteristics they demonstrate at each stage can be different from those at every other stage. It is unrealistic to expect students to be successful at tasks that require a level of cognitive ability not yet attained. If they are not ready to take on the learning, they can be set up to fail.

Connecting to and Extending Existing Knowledge, Skills, and Experience

All students have existing knowledge, skills, understandings and experiences. Teachers need to identify and activate this prior learning and link it to the work at hand. Smith and Wilhelm (2002) found that the boys in their study were most interested in reading texts that fed into their pre-existing interests. In fact, the study showed that the boys' interests were not developed through reading. The boys felt that their interests were already developed before the reading and then were supplemented through the school-related reading. In other words, in this study, the students felt that they brought the interests to school; the interests were not developed in school.

This notion presents a challenge for teachers. Teachers have to find ways to use students' prior learning as a resource for uncovering the curriculum. Beginning with students' current knowledge or interest in a topic, the key to moving forward is tweaking that interest to unlock new discoveries.

You can use a variety of strategies at the start of a unit of work, a concept, or topic lesson to identify what students already know. These strategies enable students to use and hear subject specific vocabulary. Their knowledge is reinforced and extended as they talk, listen and piggyback ideas off each other. Concept maps, K-W-L lists, even journal entries provide a wealth of information about what students know. Using anticipation and prediction activities at the start of a new topic encourages students to think about what a topic might cover. Students can refer to, compare and contrast, and/or amend their initial predictions at different stages of the unit work.

New learning occurs when thinking is challenged and extended. Adolescent learners need to be stretched (with assistance) from the edge of what they can do independently to the next point of their learning. As they are stretched, they start to build up new knowledge, understandings, and skills. Use simple strategies, such as three-level guides, directed silent reading, and developing questions, to move students from surface levels of reading and research to more advanced levels of thinking, research, and application.

Connecting to Family, Language, Cultural, and Socio-economic Experiences

The experiences students bring to school with them are often referred to as background experiences because they are mistakenly seen as not being related to the business of schooling. In fact, these experiences are central to adolescent learners' identities, and they don't disappear while students are at school. They represent a wide range of cultural, family, language, and socio-economic experiences. Learning programs need to not only link to these experiences, they also need to recruit and place them in the foreground of all learning activities.

Students need to be taught that school is just one way of talking, acting, and behaving among many that they will learn in a lifetime. Mastering one discourse, or way of talking and behaving, does not preclude participating in or learning others. The idea of embracing several discourses at once is important for English-language learners who may feel at a disadvantage with their fluently English-speaking peers. English-language learners have a particularly challenging time at school because they are trying to learn the discourse of the school (one way of talking, acting, behaving) while also trying to learn the language in which the content of school is conducted. Some English-language learners may feel disenfranchised by the school environment because their primary discourse — their native language and customs — may appear to be irrelevant and even unwanted in the school community. Teachers need to find strategies to let these students know that they do not have to abandon one discourse to learn and enjoy the benefits of others.

One way to help students avoid the either/or attitude toward school discourse is to give them examples of people who successfully juggle or practice various ways of behaving without abandoning their primary one. In other words, many people participate in multiple discourses without leaving the primary one behind. For example, many white-collar executives who live a button-down existence during the week to fit into their corporate environments don helmets and leather suits on weekends when they participate in motorcycle clubs. Similarly, people with regular day jobs play in rock bands at night and on weekends and manage to balance the two discourses without a problem. Many new Canadians are active in their cultural societies maintaining the customs and traditions of the homeland, but also fit into the mainstream of the Canadian workforce.

In all discourses — rock bands, motorcycle clubs, school — there are rules, specialized vocabulary, appropriate dress, and other aspects by which the members of the particular community identify themselves. The teacher's job is to create the environment where students can learn the principles of the particular discourse: school, English, basketball, and so on.

Connecting to Learning across Subject Areas

Students' learning outcomes improve when they are able to make links across different learning areas. Teachers can help students make those links if they work collaboratively, sharing ideas and seeing themselves as part of a team responsible for the development of all students in the school.

Hargreaves (2001) highlights the importance of finding time for teachers to work collaboratively during the school day to effect changes to practice and to successfully integrate curriculum.

- Professional collaboration [and planning collaboratively] can be an exceptionally important asset to the curriculum planning process, giving it clarity, consistency, and momentum . . . .

- The planning demands that teachers face are substantial. The time needed for planning is extensive, not perfunctory . . . [T]his planning time often needs to be spent with colleagues so that intellectual challenges can be met together.

- Job-embedded professional learning is more complex to administer organizationally and more difficulty to justify politically, as it seems to take up teachers' time from their classes. Yet . . . evidence points to its immense value for making complex change processes successful.

- Complex curriculum change depends for its success on forms of planning and professional learning that are embedded in and not appended to the fundamental work of teaching.
- [Administrators need to] make professional development time for teachers to plan, talk about, and review the changes they are undertaking together a higher priority than short, sharp in-service training sessions.
- Learning to change is intellectually demanding, and teachers need lots of time, inside and outside of the school day, to think though complex curriculum changes individually and with their colleagues.

It may be easy for some schools to become more collaborative about the way in which they work. However, for many teachers and for many schools, the issues require a lot of patience and effort and are not easy to address. Improving how schools work is something valuable to target, but it tends to happen over time. The efforts of individuals, departments, and key stakeholders are essential to achieving such reform, but it is not likely to happen immediately. In the meantime, teachers have to work within their existing school culture and organization to avoid fragmentation, duplication, and overlap, and to effect improvement in learning.

Many schools have tried different ways of organizing the learning environment to cater to the needs of adolescent learners. They have clustered students in various primary/secondary configurations, set up schools-within-schools and teaching/learning teams (thus creating communities of learners), reduced the number of teachers that students encounter, made the timetable more flexible by ensuring larger, uninterrupted blocks of time for learning, and integrated the curriculum.

Some schools continue to examine their current practice consistently to identify how their organizational structures and timetabling processes impact on students' learning. They collect data to inform the planning and implementing of strategies that minimize barriers to learning. They use this type of analysis to identify options and possibilities for engaging students in their own learning and for giving them responsibility for making decisions about their own learning programs.

Connecting to Different Learning Styles

All students have preferred learning and working styles. They might share certain approaches, but they generally retain preferences that are uniquely their own. It is easy to forget that students learn in different ways, and to plan assignments and to teach as if every student were the same. Kinesthetic or tactile learners, who make up the vast majority of the dropout rate in secondary schools, cannot sit still for long periods of time and need to move and touch things in order to effectively demonstrate their learning. They are unlikely to do well in tests and programs that reinforce a narrow range of learning styles. Individual differences therefore are important and need to be recognized and respected when planning learning programs.

Students' different learning styles need to be linked and recruited into all aspects of the curriculum. This enables them to continue to develop their strengths. Students also need to continue to build up their skills in other areas, to find out what it is like to work in different ways, and to learn to accommodate other people's learning styles.

Students can be challenged and stretched when they are expected to demonstrate their learning in different ways (i.e. through drama, art, graphs, diagrams, music, dance). They learn to accommodate and appreciate other students' ways of working when they participate in collaborative small-group work. Some do not necessarily work well in groups, and therefore consideration needs to be given to those who work best alone. Group activities that start with 10-15 minutes of individual thinking/planning time (or that build in individual reflection time at various stages of the learning programme) can provide successful learning opportunities for all students.

Accommodate different learning styles by

- encouraging *team teaching* within a subject department or school (so that all students are exposed to a range of teaching styles)

- employing *small-group work*, such as Literature Circles and jigsaw activities that allow students to utilize their strengths when contributing to group tasks

- developing thematic units in a content area in order to accommodate students' learning styles

- providing a balanced range of activities that incorporate elements of individual, small-group, or whole-class learning

Connecting to Other Students

Adolescent learners learn about the world and generate, test, refine, and extend their ideas through talk. They learn best when they are able to clarify their thinking by bouncing ideas off each other.

Students benefit from working with their peers in pairs or in small groups. Group activities provide ideal opportunities for linking and recruiting ideas. When students share their expertise and skills with their peers, they become part of a community of learners.

Bennett and Rolheiser (2001) identify key points about cooperative learning:

- Learning is socially constructed; we seldom learn isolated from others.

- Everyone in the group needs to be accountable for the learning.

- Teachers must actively teach social skills, communication, and critical thinking skills.

- Groups must understand how they function as a group.

- Group work must have worthy tasks and objectives that are appropriate for group work and face-to-face interaction.

- Groups of 2, 3 and 4 encourage interaction.

- Larger groups decrease the amount of talk time.

- Taking the time to be thoughtful about who will be working with whom will have long-term benefits (p. 141).

Connecting to Learning in Elementary Schools

Most systematic strategies highlight the importance of linking to and recruiting the ideas, perceptions, and information of elementary school teachers who have already taught the same students. Much is to be gained when the strengths and knowledge of elementary pedagogy and secondary subject-specific expertise is shared, including issues related to duplication and overlap.

Teachers often resist using material that has already been taught in earlier grades. They also tell their students that they can't refer to items that have been used in other projects, book reports, or essays. However, as Beers points out (2003, p. 118), when students re-study or re-read topics or books, they are revising their understandings of the text. Renewed study or rereading reveals an additional layer or dimension of understanding which may manifest itself in a new question, connection, or clarification.

Connecting to Others in the School Community

Student, teacher, family, and community partnerships provide powerful links that enhance learning. Learning opportunities are enhanced when a school community links to, recruits and extends the expertise, skills, support, cultural experiences, resources, facilities, business acumen, and knowledge of its members. Partnerships need to be meaningful, non-tokenistic, and proactive, with benefits for all participants.

According to Cumming (2000), schools are no longer seen as the primary producers, deliverers, and assessors of knowledge and skills. There is an increasing recognition that students need a broader education that will enable them to participate in, and also contribute to, society. Community-based learning is learning that takes place in the community, beyond the confines of the classroom and the school. It involves individuals, other than teachers, as part of the learning process. Students remain at the centre of the learning process, while maintaining connections to, and support from, teachers, parents, and other community members.

The emphasis is on cooperative planning, implementation, and evaluation of meaningful and productive work that has a strong educational focus and clearly articulated outcomes. Students are able to participate in activities that are real, rather than simulated, and they can exhibit, present, and be acknowledged for their work in community settings (p 36-39).

Making Learning Meaningful

When was the last time you heard someone claim that school education is routinely exciting, engaging and stimulating for students, that it provides the kind of rush that comes from theatre or music or competitive sport, that it regularly takes students so close to the edge of their experience that they get stage fright? When did school last seem slightly dangerous, a place that would give you a nervous thrill like the thrill you get from taking risks and going beyond your limits. In the iconography of contemporary life, school is the grey cardigan, sensible shoes, making sure you have a hanky, going to bed early, wearing clean underwear in case you get hit by a bus, and chewing each

mouthful 32 times. It is the part of Western tradition that assumes that what
you enjoy cannot be good for you, and what is good for you cannot be fun.
Schooling is…the grey cardigan and the sensible shoes compared with the
sparkle and sequins of popular culture.

(Wilson, 2000, p. 3)

Balancing Content and Processes

Making learning meaningful (or "making their heads spin" (Barber, 1999)) means more than simply making learning fun. It also means more than simply covering content. It means designing learning experiences that balance the demands between process and content expectations.

It is easy to fall into the content trap. "Covering" a body of content does not necessarily mean that students have learned the content. As Kathleen and James Strickland point out, a good teacher not "cover" anything. "Instead, he or she works to 'un-cover' the curriculum, to provide experiences that allow students to develop certain insights and an improved level of language competence or content knowledge" (1993, p. 12).

What is important is that students develop skills that will enable them to process *any* body of content at any stage in their life. In other words, students will learn how to learn to support a life-long learning habit.

Students need time to process and absorb or internalize content. They need time to listen, read, think, talk, plan, write, and reflect on and represent their learning. Learning is best demonstrated when they can apply their learning in another context. Processes matter — because they impact on the effectiveness and on the quality of the learning — but they require time. Striking a balance between the need for teachers to deliver content and for students to process information continues to be an ongoing issue in the middle- and secondary-school context.

As part of a solution to this issue, some schools have conducted a subject or school audit of what is taught at each year level. They determined what content was mandated and was therefore non-negotiable, and they identified what content could be compacted or removed. They examined what was happening across the school to ensure that content was not being repeated, and in doing so, determined that responsibility for teaching a particular concept could be shared between teachers from different subject areas. (This exercise could be extended to include feeder elementary schools.)

Contextualizing the Learning

When learning is contextualized and relevant, it becomes meaningful. Adolescent learners like to know why and how information learned at school will be useful to them. When they know why the information is being taught, how it fits into the bigger world, and how it links to their own life, they are more likely to take the learning on board. When what they learn is relevant for work (and future work), relevant to them and to their family, and relevant to the wider world around them (Hargreaves, 1998), it is meaningful. Adolescent learners love to learn real things. They want to be part of life in the real world. They like to be doing things that they deem to be important, or things that link to their own experiences. The more direct or hands-on the experience is, the better. If the real thing is not an option, then indirect, vicarious, or simulated experiences also allow them to feel that they are close to the action. These kinds of experiences provide a context within which learning can occur, as well as a shared experience that can be used as a stimulus for language and knowledge extension and enrichment.

When learning takes place in contexts outside the classroom (in the workplace, a church, museum, or shopping centre) students are able to observe ways of behaving, ways of speaking, and conventions that are particular to certain situations. They quickly learn to adapt their own language and behaviour according to purpose and audience. This "on-site" learning can be more meaningful than learning conducted in an isolated classroom, away from the real action.

Many students need to explore, discuss, mind-map, brainstorm, or research a topic before they are able to write about it effectively. These types of before activities prepare students for the work that is to follow. They provide background information and content about which students can write.

Students are more likely to write, perform, and design well if they see the processes involved in writing, designing, organizing, and performing modelled, and if they encounter examples of good writing, designing, organizing, and performing. When they encounter high-quality products of those processes, they can visualize their goals. Time spent on before and during activities such as these is not wasted, because this type of careful preparation ensures that their learning outcomes (after) are improved.

Keeping it Relevant, Engaging, and Motivational

Adolescent learners relish autonomy. They become energized when they determine or negotiate learning goals, when they are interested in the research topics to be investigated, when those topics are of interest and of use to them now or in the future, when they are given real problems to solve, and when they are able to negotiate both the nature of the learning task and the assessment regime.

Students enjoy planning and working independently. They also enjoy working collaboratively with others. They thrive on being active and self-directed in their approaches to learning tasks.

When reflection time is built into all learning activities, learning is further enhanced. Teachers reinforce the message that they have trust in their students' ability when they recognize that there are many paths to learning and when they are prepared to act as facilitators for learning, rather than always being the "one who knows."

Adolescent learners like to be part of what is current or topical. Classroom programs that utilize media, television, CD ROMs, films, and other forms of digital and learning technologies are more likely to engage students' interest. When the learning program incorporates, links to, recruits, or extends current issues, human-interest stories, or politics, it allows students to build knowledge about a topic from a range of sources. Topical news broadcasts, feature articles, films, comic strips, or the newspaper can become rich and motivating sources of topic for discussion, debate, or research. Students will often listen, talk, read, write, and think critically — without being aware that they are learning — because they become so engrossed in the task or topic. When teachers know their students well, they are able to recognize what is of interest and use this interest as the basis for learning. Beane (1991) suggests that it is in middle school that the curriculum should focus on widely shared concerns of early adolescents and the larger world, rather than on "increasing specialization and differentiation among separate subjects."

Rapid changes in technology mean that students can locate information from across the world, via fax, e-mail, chat rooms, bulletin boards, and so on. How much better to be able to ask students in other countries or contexts direct questions about their life; to be able to make contact with a real nuclear scientist or renowned explorer by fax or e-mail.

Adolescent learners enjoy working collaboratively in small groups. Debating, in particular, is an excellent strategy for engaging students in purposeful, relevant, and motivational learning. It requires research work, planning and preparation, time-keeping skills, formal language, a requirement to match recognized conventions, and the ability to practise speaking at length on any given topic, in public.

Similarly, collaborative activities such as writing to the community paper about a local issue; creating board games; rewriting a chapter of a subject-specific book in student-friendly terms; setting up worm farms, an herb garden or a school environmental centre; developing a multimedia presentation advertising the school; re-writing a chapter of a mathematics text for younger students; designing a local shopping centre or a solar car; writing and presenting a play about a health issue; writing a restaurant review; designing a school Web page; designing a playground for the local kindergarten; making up subject-specific lyrics to a well known melody; creating quizzes and competitions; setting up a school radio station; developing a group picture book on a subject-specific topic; or constructing a newspaper for a particular audience are all student-centred activities that provide a motivational stimulus for learning.

Teachers become valuable resource persons, coaches, leaders and guides, as well as experts and authorities, when they generate a broad range of stimulating and contextualised learning environments.

(Schools Council, Australia, 1992)

Teachers use their professional judgment when planning learning programs. They must decide if and/or when a traditional approach might be more appropriate for a particular group of students, or for teaching a particular type of skill. They must also decide whether other approaches might provide variety, suit the needs of a group of students, or achieve particular learning outcomes. Some teachers use integrated programs that allow students to demonstrate outcomes across a range of curriculum areas. They find these minimize the risk of overlapping between different subject areas. Variations of such programs include having teachers from different learning areas plan units of work collaboratively around a concept, but teach their subject-specific component in their own learning area. Alternatively, they can involve learning teams or teachers from different learning areas collaboratively planning, implementing, and assessing cross curriculum integrated or interdisciplinary programs or tasks.

Most agree that the curriculum should not be integrated simply for the sake of integrating, and that such a step works best when integrating subjects is more likely to ensure that students will achieve particular learning outcomes. Better results are obtained if "big" concepts, rather than smaller themes or interesting (but random) activities, are used, and if integrated approaches are tackled for part of a day or week, rather than for longer periods of time. It is important not to integrate too many subjects within the one program, and to know that some learning areas do not always integrate naturally with others (for example, languages other than English with mathematics). "Forced fits" are rarely successful. When open-ended learning tasks are incorporated within integrated programs, students are able to enter and exit tasks at different points and demonstrate their learning in various ways.

Some of the issues related to curriculum integration can be minimized by dedicating explicit teaching time to the skills and content specific to each learning area and identifying measurable target learning outcomes. Students need to be made aware of the essential elements of each discipline that make up the integrated program. When it comes to assessment, teachers have found that it is best to use subject-specific rubrics or assessment tools that they have developed themselves. These usually incorporate key outcomes from each of the target learning areas. Other outcomes demonstrated by students can be noted for future teaching and learning programs.

Other teachers have tried negotiating an integrated curriculum, using the Beane and Brodhagen (1995) process. This requires students to reflect on questions they have about themselves and the world, to share and put in priority their questions at the small- or whole-group level, and to vote on the selection and order of topics/ themes to be addressed. Teachers add supplementary questions to extend and address gaps in the theme/topic, and students then identify the types of tasks that would enable them to answer their questions. Teachers or teaching teams co-ordinate the sequencing, resourcing, and timetabling of the integrated curriculum and build in regular conferences or debriefing sessions with individuals or small groups of students. According to Beane (1991), this shift in focus from teacher to student redefines the role of the teacher from "gatekeeper of knowledge" to facilitator and guide.

> *The spin-offs from student participation in curriculum are many, and schools are only beginning to understand the immense resource that is made available when students' energy and interest is used constructively for their own and one another's benefit.*
>
> (Brennan and Sachs, 1998, p. 16)

Setting Horizons and Providing Explicit Feedback

Adolescent learners need a sense of control, a challenge, unambiguous goals, feedback, and clearly identified reasons for studying or reading about a particular topic. They need the skills to accomplish the task so that they can feel competent and experience the satisfaction that comes from understanding the process and being in control. They need to know the expectations and the outcomes at the beginning and end of a unit of work or lesson so that they can define the target they are trying to reach. And they need to know that the target has a practical pay-off in terms of its importance as a building block to learning something else, or as an end in itself.

They also need to know how they will reach the target outcomes. Setting targets, or establishing a purpose, is similar to deciding on a destination. Unless students know where they are going, why they are going, and how they are going to get there, the journey is likely to be aimless. The destination and journey have to be worthwhile, just as any trip has to have been worth the effort of getting there. They need a map, which means providing them with a reasonable challenge (target/outcome) and the appropriate skills to meet the challenge. It is essential that the target outcomes and purposes for activities or programs are articulated before and summarized after each lesson or program of work.

Students also need to have ongoing (formative) and constructive feedback to keep them informed about their progress toward the target. This lets them know how they are doing. The feedback should highlight explicitly what students have done well, and highlight what they can do to ensure further progress.

Adolescents are sophisticated learners. They are more likely to commit to programs that allow them some autonomy. They enjoy planning, organizing, implementing, and evaluating pathways of learning that have been negotiated with their teachers. Student-centred approaches favour asking students to identify aspects of their work that they are pleased with, as well as aspects they feel they need help with, and then negotiating follow-up strategies collaboratively. The degree of negotiation might range from a single task within a program to complete freedom of choice, depending on the students' needs, abilities, and interests, and depending on the teacher's comfort level. Students' self-esteem is raised when teachers indicate that they are confident in their ability to manage aspects of their own learning.

Motivation for adolescent learners is often the enjoyment or thrill of the immediate experience. As they identify learning targets and negotiate methods to reach them, students need to see how the target is going to help them with the next step in the process, or what they can do once they reach the target. Therefore, an end product of some kind is important. Adolescent learners in particular need opportunities to do something concrete with their new knowledge or information — prepare a demonstration, act out a skit, role-play, write a report, prepare a pamphlet, draw a map, construct a model, design a Web site, teach the material to others, send a letter to the editor, and so on.

While it may seem a paradox, adolescent learners need both the challenge of working under pressure to achieve high standards and time to reflect on their learning, so that they can define and internalize new and difficult concepts. At this stage in their development adolescents become more self-aware as learners and need to be challenged to "think about their thinking;" about how they learn and what works best for them as learners.

Moving Them Forward

The middle and secondary phase of schooling is often regarded as being rather "aimless" because it falls in between the phases of schooling that are considered to really matter. As an antidote to this students need to recognize that they are making progress with their learning. The key issue is to support their learning without losing sight of the necessity to develop independent learners.

Supporting Learning

All students require support to move from one level to the next. They need to be challenged and stretched from the edge of what they can do independently to the next stage of their learning.

The zone between what the learner has currently achieved, and what they can potentially achieve (with assistance) is called the "zone of proximal development (ZPD)" (Vygotsky, 1978).

> *The assistance that is necessary to learning in the ZPD allows the learner to appropriate the problem-solving language and strategies of the more expert person who is lending the learner assistance. When the expert's knowledge has been internalized and used by the learner, then competence is visibly enhanced.*
>
> (Smith and Wilhelm, p. 103)

The behaviours that students demonstrate at each stage inform decisions about the selection of strategies that will best support them to make further progress toward target outcomes or attainment levels. Strategies for adolescent students need to be appropriate for their development level.

Even students who demonstrate high learning outcomes need to be supported. Those, for instance, who demonstrate outstanding computer skills still require support to continue to make progress whereas those just starting to experiment with a computer keyboard will need support of a different kind.

Students, adults, or teachers can provide support at the different points that lead to the mastery of a concept or skill. It is not necessary to provide the same support at the whole-class level unless, of course, all students in the class are learning a new skill at the same time.

Show Me, Help Me, Let Me

Adolescent learners need the support of scaffolding strategies to stretch to the next phase of their learning.

> *Vygotskian instruction goes through a process of modeling (Show Me), of assistance in which expertise is gradually handed over to the student (Help Me), and then observation as the student independently uses the learned strategies in a meaningful context (Let Me).*
>
> (Smith and Wilhelm, p. 130)

The use of training wheels on a bicycle is an example of scaffolding. The young person has seen how others ride bicycles (Show Me). Training wheels (Help Me) are used until the cyclist practices riding the bicycle independently, becomes more confident as he/she experiences success. When the wheels are removed (Let Me), it is a sign that learning has taken place and is a mark of progress.

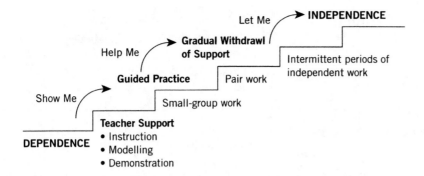

When selecting scaffolding strategies, it is important to determine:

- who needs support (because it is frustrating for students to have to complete scaffolding activities if they don't really need them)
- what kind of support is most appropriate
- how long the support is needed

A supply of mini-lessons to assist students in the Show Me or Help Me stages is recommended. These might be used with individuals or small groups of students who need selected teaching or re-teaching of concepts or procedures.

Support or scaffolding strategies can be put in place for as long as they are required, but need to be removed or varied once they are no longer appropriate. The gradual release of scaffolding places the final responsibility for learning on the student.

Types of scaffolding can vary, but generally include strategies such as:

Immersion	Models or examples are provided so that students become familiar with the text or item and can identify common patterns, structures, or features.
Explicit Teaching and Feedback	The teacher explicitly explains the steps involved in a process and provides ongoing, explicit feedback as students "approximate" the task.
Modelling and Demonstrating	The teacher demonstrates and talks through a process so that students can hear the thinking that others go through as they tackle a particular task.
Guided Reading or Viewing	The teacher uses strategies such as focus questions at before, during, and after stages of the reading task, or note-making frameworks, to help students navigate and understand the content and structure of print and non-print texts.

(continued)

Guided Writing	The teacher supports individuals, pairs, or groups of students as they tentatively compose a piece of writing. Use strategies such as explicit teaching, peer-assessment, and writing frameworks as needed.
Joint Construction	The teacher and students share ideas and jointly construct a piece of work (for example, writing, note-making, graphs, diagramming) using the overhead projector or board.

When teachers know where their students are in relation to target learning outcomes, and when they understand the purpose of particular strategies and know how they work, they are able to select strategies that help students make progress from one level of learning to another.

Introducing Literacy Strategies in the Classroom

Teachers need to be familiar with a wide range of strategies and practices that they can use to cater to the diversity associated with adolescent abilities and interests. Strategies can't be taught once and immediately learned. They need to be explained and modelled explicitly several times before students can apply them independently. Students need to know why they are using a strategy and how, when, and where to apply it. They also need to have multiple opportunities to practise and develop strategies so that they can use those strategies throughout their life.

In a strategies-rich classroom, it is useful to teach one or two strategies and to build up the repertoire slowly. You can teach strategies explicitly and model them in both small- and large-group instruction and in one-to–one teaching situations. Continue explicit explanations, modelling, ongoing guidance, and explicit feedback as students practise using the strategies.

Instructions should include explanations about when and where to apply particular strategies, as well as the benefits associated with using various strategies. Prompt students through questioning techniques to think about additional or possible ways to extend and expand their use of strategies. Highlight the ways in which different students apply strategies to the same content and invite individual students to explain why (and how) they used a particular strategy to complete a piece of work (Pressley, 2000).

The aim is to make students aware of the ways in which different strategies can help them learn more effectively, and for them to be able to self-select and apply them confidently in different contexts and for different purposes.

Selecting Appropriate Strategies

Be careful when selecting strategies because inappropriate selection can detract from learning experiences. The "grab bag" approach to selecting strategies is not effective. Each strategy has a particular purpose. Some support learning. Some provide organizational structures. Others facilitate comprehension.

Each strategy suits different kinds of tasks and achieves different purposes. Students do not learn skills and concepts in the same way; some strategies support the teaching of skills; some support the teaching of concepts.

Some strategies are flexible and can be used equally well at before, during, and after stages of a lesson or unit of work. When selecting learning strategies, it is always valuable to plan from the after stage first. This means identifying target learning outcomes first, because this information drives decisions about the kinds of strategies you put in place to help students achieve those outcomes.

Strategies for Concepts and for Skills

Students do not learn skills and concepts in the same way. Some strategies teach skills and some teach concepts; different strategies are appropriate at different times.

Concepts are best taught by building up layers of understanding, starting from the knowledge that students already possess. As students assimilate new knowledge they form new understandings. Strategies suitable for teaching concepts allow students to move between overall generalizations and details, and to explore links between subject-specific information and their own world.

These strategies, among others, facilitate the teaching of concepts:

Three-Level Guides promote critical thinking and internalization of concepts.

Journal Writing facilitates reflection and recording of understandings.

Group Work provides opportunities for active participation in clarifying and refining ideas.

Pros, Cons, and Questions facilitates synthesis of other points of view on a topic.

Skills, on the other hand, need to be taught explicitly. Strategies such as modelling the skill, and collaborative activities, such as guided writing and joint construction, are very effective. It is important to determine how many sub-skills are involved in each task and to identify the order and rate at which to teach these sub-skills.

These strategies, among others, facilitate the teaching of skills:

Joint Construction, in which teacher and students collaboratively construct a piece of writing

Guided Writing, in which the linguistic (language) features and conventions of a text are made clear through modelling

Skimming, in which students are explicitly taught how to gain a general impression or overview of a text quickly

Scanning, in which students are explicitly taught how to locate specific details quickly

Spoon-feeding versus Independence

Teachers frequently make the majority of decisions about tasks to be completed in class, selecting strategies, activities, and evaluation methods. This can mean losing valuable opportunities for students to use thinking skills to determine which writing framework or note-making structure might be more appropriate; to practise the skills involved in selecting appropriate strategies for particular tasks; to develop the skills of time management; and to develop the skills required to be independent, self-regulating learners. When teachers make all the decisions about what is to happen in the classroom, students are also denied valuable opportunities to make confident, informed choices about the purpose and appropriateness of different strategies for particular activities. They can get used to being "spoon-fed," and quickly become dependent learners (Kiddey, 1998).

On the other hand, some students simply do not have the developmental, organizational, or self-management skills required to complete their work independently. They cannot be left to take responsibility for managing their learning, because they still need help.

There is a fine line, then, between knowing who to support, when to support them, how to support them, and when to wean them off the support. The only way that teachers can effectively gauge how students are progressing with their learning is to monitor their processes, products, and performances over a period of time, in a range of different contexts, and to alter the teaching and learning program accordingly.

Making Sure They're Learning

Assessment

If the prime responsibility of teachers "is not to teach, but to ensure that students learn" (Dimmock, 1991) then the prime purpose of assessment is to ensure that learning has taken place. Teachers need to know what their students know and can do, in relation to learning outcomes. They can then put in place a learning program that will enable students to make further progress. A further purpose of assessment is to be able to report on student competence and achievement.

Over the past several years, with the increased focus on the importance of assessment and the advent of resources such as *First Steps*, there has been a stronger emphasis on integrating assessment, learning, and teaching.

The principles that apply for learning and teaching and the learning emphases for adolescents need to apply directly to assessment as well. Assessment should be all of the following:

Valid	Assessment should provide valid information on the actual ideas, processes, products, and values expected of students.
Educative	Assessment should make a positive contribution to student learning.
Explicit	Assessment criteria should be explicit so that the basis for judgments is clear and public.

Fair	Assessme~~As~~ be demonstrably fair to all students and not discri~~~~ grounds that are irrelevant to the achieveme~~~~ omes
Comprehensive	Judgment~~~~ nt progress should be based on multiple k~~ius and~~ sources of evidence.

Improving the Assessment Regime

Assessment in middle and secondary school tends to be formal and does not always match well with adolescents' learning characteristics or with the teaching and learning emphases required for this group of learners.

Assessment "refers to a collection of data, information that enlightens the teacher and the learner, information that drives instruction. Good teachers assess constantly, performing the first stage of a recursive process. They observe what is happening in their classrooms – 'kid-watching' as Yetta Goodman (1978) would say – and then talk to students and ask them questions about their learning. . . They devise ways to record their observations. They also share their assessment with their students, so students can adjust their performances to meet criteria for personal expectations or those imposed on them by their teachers or by others" (Strickland, p. 19).

Assessment should reflect, encourage, and be an integral part of good instruction. Teachers identify assessment strategies as part of their lesson and unit planning. What do they want students to know? What skills will students need to learn? What behaviours will the new learning change? What aspirations or motivations will be necessary to engage student learning? Are there attitudes to the material that will affect students' learning of it? How will teachers assess these things as the unit unfolds?

Formative assessment is designed to provide direction for improvement and/or to adjust the program. This means that teachers assess primarily to ensure that students learn better, and so that the teachers can adjust their own performances to help students learn more effectively.

Being able to self-monitor and to self-evaluate are essential skills that successful writers, thinkers, problem-solvers, readers, and others do constantly. An effective assessment system shows, helps, and lets students take responsibility for their own self-reflection.

Teachers use multiple measures for assessment, examining students' growth from various perspectives. They need a rich repertoire of assessment strategies in designing sensitive and appropriate evaluation activities which will lead to grades. Among these activities are portfolios, peer assessments, conferences, demonstrations of learning, tests, and projects (Daniels and Bizar, 2001, p. 220).

Summative assessment is designed to provide information to be used in making judgments about a student's achievement at the end of a period of instruction. Summative assessments often include culminating activities — demonstrations, projects, seminars, models, and so on.

Evaluation "is the product of [formative and summative] assessment, a step further toward understanding and drawing conclusions. After gathering data — information and evidence — teachers, like researchers, must put the pieces together, evaluating the products of their efforts and the progress of their students. This evaluation is neither subjective — an opinion based on what the teacher instinctively feels — nor simply an average of scores. Rather, evaluation uses a variety of assessment techniques and validates its conclusions by investigating relationships in the data, triangulating the data, analyzing what is gathered from a multiplicity of perspectives. Evaluation in this sense is helpful to learners rather than simply judgmental, understandable rather than mysterious, and anticipated by learners when they have been informed and involved in the assessment process" (Strickland, p. 20).

Grades are an inevitable aspect of public schooling. They are part of the recursive process of assessment and evaluation. Sooner or later, students' achievement must be represented by a symbol — a grade. Grades are, therefore, primarily a communication tool. Students, parents, school administrators, post-secondary institutions, and employers all want clear information on student achievement, and assume that grades reflect some kind of accuracy.

> *Achievement demonstrates knowledge, skills, and behaviour that are stated as learning objectives [target outcomes] for a course or unit of instruction. . . Grades are limited to individual achievement and are not used as punishment for poor attendance, inappropriate behaviour, or lack of punctuality.*
> (O'Connor, 1999, p. 40)

Grades are nothing more than symbols that summarize achievement. They must reflect actual student performance based on publicly available criterion-referenced standards, not artificially determined mark distributions. They are the distillation of a recursive process of assessment — formative and summative — and of the evaluation process. If grades are a representation of achievement to the student, parents, and community, then assessment processes must reflect substantial evidence that the grades are accurate.

Improving the Variety and Range of Assessments

If learning experiences are to be varied and challenging, so too must the assessment. An expanded range of broad, well designed assessment tasks should provide opportunities for observation and assessment of performance, and the collection of hard and soft data for individual and group work. These should reflect the spread of needs and interests of students in each classroom.

Teachers know a great deal about their students' learning. They gain rich information about behaviour, performance, strengths, and weaknesses by observing students at work. They can collect multiple kinds of evidence from many sources to help them assess students' achievement. As mentioned earlier, teachers devise many ways to record their observations and share them with their students.

A wide range of assessments — observations, projects, group work, Literature Circles, portfolios, teacher-made tests, writing assignments — is balanced against decontextualized measures: standardized tests and formal examinations to arrive at an evaluation of a student's achievement. The evaluation becomes the grade that is communicated to the student, parents, and administration.

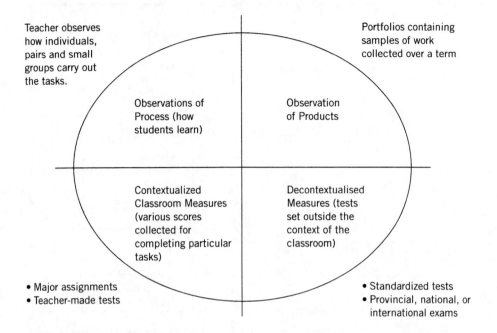

Teacher observes how individuals, pairs and small groups carry out the tasks.

Portfolios containing samples of work collected over a term

Observations of Process (how students learn)

Observation of Products

Contextualized Classroom Measures (various scores collected for completing particular tasks)

Decontextualised Measures (tests set outside the context of the classroom)

• Major assignments
• Teacher-made tests

• Standardized tests
• Provincial, national, or international exams

Adapted by permission from *Evaluating Literacy* by Robert J. Anthony, Terry D. Johnson, Norma I. Mickelson, and Alison Preece. Copyright © 1991 by Heinemann Books, Ltd. Published by Heinemann, a division of Reed Elsevier, Inc., Portsmouth, NH. All rights reserved.

Constructing Purposeful Assessment

Adolescents are not particularly accepting of the ritual of formal assessments. They are much more accepting of formative assessment that reflects their growth in contexts that are considered to be "life-like." As mentioned, there are multiple kinds and sources of evidence to use to monitor students' learning. The range of assessment methods that teachers may use includes some of the following tools.

1. Student portfolios are collections of students' work that connect separate items to form clearer and fuller pictures of each student as a learner. They are a valid and reliable source of evidence to use in assembling data about students' achievement over time. Portfolios show students' ability to apply their skills in a range of situations. They can be used to demonstrate evidence that incremental steps of progress are being made. Portfolios can be used in one learning area, or can include work across a range of learning areas.

Different types of portfolios serve different purposes:

■ Inside a Portfolio

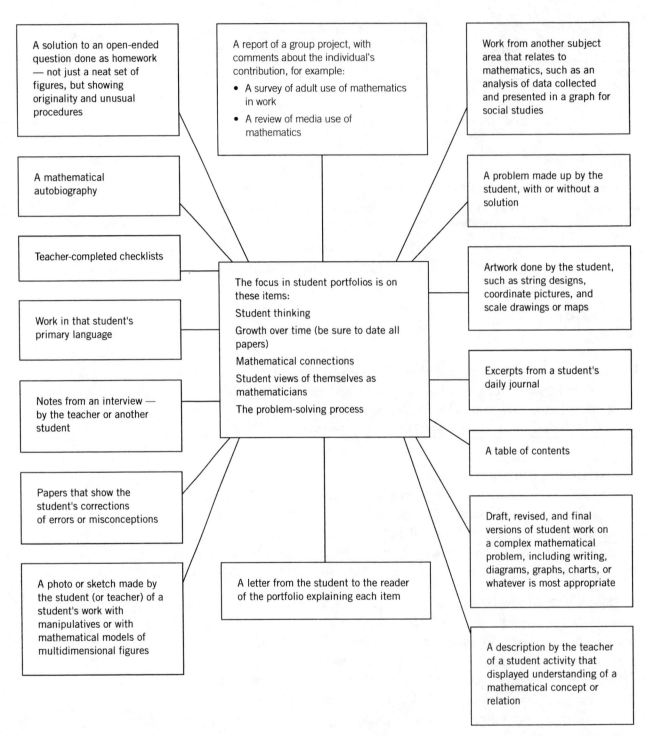

A solution to an open-ended question done as homework — not just a neat set of figures, but showing originality and unusual procedures

A mathematical autobiography

Teacher-completed checklists

Work in that student's primary language

Notes from an interview — by the teacher or another student

Papers that show the student's corrections of errors or misconceptions

A photo or sketch made by the student (or teacher) of a student's work with manipulatives or with mathematical models of multidimensional figures

A report of a group project, with comments about the individual's contribution, for example:
- A survey of adult use of mathematics in work
- A review of media use of mathematics

The focus in student portfolios is on these items:

Student thinking

Growth over time (be sure to date all papers)

Mathematical connections

Student views of themselves as mathematicians

The problem-solving process

A letter from the student to the reader of the portfolio explaining each item

Work from another subject area that relates to mathematics, such as an analysis of data collected and presented in a graph for social studies

A problem made up by the student, with or without a solution

Artwork done by the student, such as string designs, coordinate pictures, and scale drawings or maps

Excerpts from a student's daily journal

A table of contents

Draft, revised, and final versions of student work on a complex mathematical problem, including writing, diagrams, graphs, charts, or whatever is most appropriate

A description by the teacher of a student activity that displayed understanding of a mathematical concept or relation

Reprinted with permission from *Mathematics Assessment: Myths, Models, Good Questions, and Practical Suggestions,* © 1991 by the National Council of Teachers of Mathematics.

Working portfolios contain sketches, notes, half-finished drafts, and completed work. These provide an interactive context for ongoing instruction and feedback.

Documentary portfolios contain collections of students' work assembled specifically for assessment. They contain not only final products of student work, but also evidence of the processes that students used to develop those products: outlines, rough drafts, brainstorming notes, sketches, and so on.

Show portfolios contain selections of materials designed to reflect the best of student work. Students use teacher-directed or negotiated criteria to select the items, and provide a reflection on each of their choices.

Portfolio assignments provide visible evidence that students are making progress. They are particularly useful for students who need a longer time to move from one level to the next because they demonstrate multiple sources of evidence of achievement: teacher observations, checklists, student drafts, journal writing examples, self- and peer-assessment sheets, audio and video tapes of student work, sketches, rough notes, research notes, brainstorming sheets, and so on.

The criteria for portfolio assessment should alter as tasks, demands, and student understandings change. Purpose statements and "road maps" or guides can lead the reader through the portfolio. Captions or statements attached to each document are also helpful because these can describe what the document is, why it is included, and what learning outcomes it demonstrates.

Portfolios also require reflective statements to summarize documents in the portfolio and to articulate what has been learned (Master and Forster, 1996).

Purpose of Portfolios

Portfolios may provide different purposes as students move through middle and secondary school. The chart below demonstrates how to use portfolios as one measure of assessment to track student growth and achievement throughout students' middle- and high-school years.

Grade	Purpose	Audience
Grades 7 and 8	• To demonstrate the learning process • To develop skills of reflection and self-evaluation • To encourage goal-setting • To communicate with parents • To demonstrate achievement	Students Parents Other schools
Grade 9	• To demonstrate the learning process • To develop skills of reflection and self-assessment • To encourage goal-setting • To communicate with parents • To demonstrate achievement	Students Parents
Grade 10	• To demonstrate the learning process • To develop skills of reflection and self-evaluation, including realistically evaluating own strengths and interests in terms of future subject and study path choices • To encourage goal-setting with longer term goals becoming more significant • To communicate with parents • To collect documentation useful in career/ education placing • To demonstrate achievement	Students Parents
Grades 11 and 12	• To collect samples of and demonstrate best work produced in each learning area • To collect documentation useful in career planning and in interviews • To set goals, both long- and short-term • To facilitate reflection and self-evaluation • To communicate with parents • To demonstrate achievement	Employers Further study institutions Career advisers Parents Student

2. Peer assessment encourages students to make decisions about their peers' performance based on explicit criteria that are jointly negotiated or pre-determined.

3. Student/teacher conferences involve students and teachers in joint negotiations about performance and follow-up action.

4. Performance assessment focuses on students' performances or products that are used to demonstrate the degree to which students can apply and demonstrate their learning.

5. Authentic assessment refers to tasks and demonstrations that are real and meaningful to the student in today's world. Skills and knowledge in school may be assessed the same way as they are in the real world. These include projects and demonstrations that involve presentations to, or feedback from, real audiences outside the school.

6. Projects, reports, and assignments encourage students to engage in in-class and/or out-of-class research activities, and may form one of the summative assessment measures for a unit or program.

7. Open-ended assessment tasks provide different entry points and points of assessment integrated within the task. Teaching can be targeted at the point of need as students work at their own rate and ability. Open-ended tasks are usually problem-solving tasks. They provide opportunities for students to demonstrate their skills and knowledge, to use their different learning styles, and to exhibit different learning outcomes. They also provide opportunities for developing and refining creative thinking and problem-solving skills. Assessment criteria for open-ended tasks need to cater to a range of ability levels. The criteria do not always have to be fixed in advance. Students may show higher levels of understandings or outcomes that were not originally part of the task. Note these for future reference and as part of other ongoing formative assessments.

8. Rubrics and marking keys provide students with the criteria that the teacher uses for assessment. When students know goals and assessments in advance, their work reflects what they know and can do. Such assessments reflect students' achievement against criterion-referenced norms rather than guesswork at hidden or unknown measurement criteria.

Rubrics and marking keys help teachers to

- set clear guidelines
- assess content objectives and student outcomes
- provide detailed feedback to students
- assist students to improve their performances over previous efforts

Rubrics and marking keys help students to

- stay on task
- know the criteria for the assignment
- improve on previous work
- monitor their own progress toward the target outcomes

Here are some examples of rubrics and marking keys.

■ Marking Key for Interviewing

Topic: _____ Date: _____
Name of Interviewer: _____ Name of Interviewee: _____

A Content – 4 marks

1. Displays good evidence of research.
2. Constructs effective open-ended questions.
3. Questions display a good understanding of issues/topic.
4. Listens actively and constructs questions arising from comments made by interviewee.

A Content – 4 marks

1. Displays good evidence of research.
2. Demonstrates a good understanding of topic/issues.
3. Supports ideas with appropriate examples and details.
4. Answers questions effectively.

B Manner – 4 marks

5. Confident manner.
6. Speaks clearly and audibly.
7. Gives appropriate body messages to interviewee.
8. Pace of delivery is appropriate.

B Manner – 4 marks

5. Answers questions confidently.
6. Speaks clearly and audibly.
7. Gives appropriate body messages to interviewee.
8. Pace of delivery is appropriate.

C Method (Structure) – 2 marks

9. Interview contains a clear introduction.
10. Asks questions in a logical order.

TOTAL: ___

C Method (Structure) – 2 marks

9. Orders answers logically.
10. Keeps answers brief and addresses important ideas.

TOTAL: ___

Adjudicator:

© Western Australian Minister of Education and Training, 2006.
Copyright restricted to purchasing school for classroom use.

Stepping Out, Reading and Viewing: Teacher's Resource 155

page 155

■ Marking Key for Debating

Grade: _____
Class: _____
Topic: _____
Date: _____

	Affirmative			Negative		
Names:	1st	2nd	3rd	1st	2nd	3rd
	0 1 2	0 1 2	0 1 2	0 1 2	0 1 2	0 1 2

Content – 8 marks

1. The arguments used appeal to the average, reasonable person.
2. Displays a thorough understanding of the topic.
3. Develops arguments well and supports them with appropriate examples.
4. 1st speakers: Clearly define topic. Other speakers: Refute opposition's arguments effectively.

Manner – 8 marks

1. Speaker is clear and audible.
2. Maintains good eye contact with audience, keeps notes unobtrusive.
3. Effective pace of delivery
4. Confident and persuasive manner

Method – 4 marks

1. Speech was clearly organized into a beginning, a well-developed middle, and an end.
2. Made good use of time.
3. Showed evidence of the roles of different speakers (bonus mark).

Individual's Total (20)
Total Team Points (60)

156 Stepping Out, Reading and Viewing: Teacher's Resource

© Western Australian Minister of Education and Training, 2006.
Copyright restricted to purchasing school for classroom use.

page 156

9. Progress maps record students' achievement patterns over time. Students follow unique patterns of growth in any area of learning. Although these patterns are not age related, teachers can draw generalizations from them and observe and record milestones on a progress map. Continuums of development, levels, and institutionalized rubrics are all examples of progress maps. Most describe behaviours as various stages and incorporate a combination of descriptions of student learning and student work samples.

Some progress maps, such as outcome statements, reflect "big picture" or global descriptions intended for systemic, summative judgments. Others, such as *First Steps* developmental continuum, use fine-grained descriptions that can be used for diagnostic purposes. Some students take a long time to move across "bigger picture" maps, and therefore teachers might prefer to use finer-grained information to indicate that students are making small, incremental steps of progress towards outcome levels.

10. Direct observation is useful when students are actively engaged in a performance, production, literature circle, presentation, or process. Record observational information on informal running records or a retrieval chart, or against a pre-determined checklist of criteria.

11. Tests measure a sample of student performance at a particular point in time under standardized conditions. It is important to keep in mind that traditional testing methods can be useful, but that they can be narrow in scope, and do not always allow students to demonstrate their wide range of skills. They do not always allow for different learning styles or unexpected responses. Further, teachers recognize that different students process knowledge and skills at different rates. Thus it is important to measure the quality, not the speed, of the performance. Additionally, reflective learners and slow writers often receive lower grades than they deserve as a result of being required to perform inappropriately time-limited assessments.

12. Checklists make it easy for teachers to identify whether or not students are able to demonstrate particular learning outcomes. The lists can be prepared in advance, and should identify a clear set of criteria to which both teacher and students can refer. The criteria can be jointly negotiated. Each time the teacher observes a targeted skill, he or she marks the appropriate criteria. Allocate space for writing informal comments alongside students' names. It is important for the teacher to be as unobtrusive as possible while observing students and/or small groups as they work, and to allow time between observations to make notes and synthesize the information. Keep checklists as they are a valuable resource for revising learning programs, when talking to parents, and when writing reports about individual students.

Checklists such as these provide an opportunity to note students' cooperative learning skills, as well as their skills and understanding in a particular learning area.

■ **Observation of Small-Group Reading Practices**

Topic: _____   Class: _____
Grade: _____   Date: _____

Task: Vocabulary in context

Students' Names						
The students were able to	Y/N	Y/N	Y/N	Y/N	Y/N	Y/N
1. Scan the text effectively	Y/N	Y/N	Y/N	Y/N	Y/N	Y/N
2. Read around the words in order to find clues for their meaning	Y/N	Y/N	Y/N	Y/N	Y/N	Y/N
3. Identify and transfer clues to the *Vocabulary in Context* sheet	Y/N	Y/N	Y/N	Y/N	Y/N	Y/N
4. Transfer the meaning into their own words	Y/N	Y/N	Y/N	Y/N	Y/N	Y/N
5. Justify their interpretation of the meaning	Y/N	Y/N	Y/N	Y/N	Y/N	Y/N

■ **Observation Checklist**

Names of Group Members	Group Processes			Subject Understandings		
	Asks to clarify/ obtain further information	Explains individual feelings/ ideas	Interrupts/a rgues politely	Understands the necessity of selecting the same unit when comparing two things	Choose suitable and uniform units	Uses a unit consistently and carefully to measure and compare
	Yes/No	Yes/No	Yes/No	Yes/No	Yes/No	Yes/No
Matt S			Tends to talk too much when others are speaking.			
Tonya						
Phuong						
Daniel						

Use a checkmark each time you observe a student at work.

An Overview of Assessment Strategies

These tools are referenced, and examples given, with each strategy in the program.

Tool	Example
1. Self-assessment A valid and valuable source of information that takes into account students' perspectives on a task or process, what they understand, and what confuses them. May take the form of a checklist, oral reflection, reflective journal writing, or a conference log recording a student/teacher interview.	I can't understand this book; it's too hard… I know how to write topic sentences but I still don't know how to develop and support my ideas.
2. Peer assessment Students can be trained to evaluate their peers effectively against specific criteria.	The ideas in your essay are clearly organized but your essay ends too suddenly.
3. Teacher notes Observational notes about students' learning behaviour and understandings	Trevor seems to have difficulty answering inferential questions.

4. Data-driven decisions Evaluating students' products and processes over time and in a variety of contexts; students' outcomes are measured against a continuum or sequence of outcomes.

A sequence of student outcomes	Level One	Level Two	Level Three	Level Four	Level Five
	——	——	——	——	——
	——	——	——	——	——
	——	——	——	——	——

5. Criteria checklists A planned observation record of achievement of specific criteria; the teacher records observed student outcomes.

Criteria to be observed:	May	Atif	Mark	Kichi
1.	✔	✔	✗	✔
2.	✔	✔	✗	✔
3.	✗	✔	✗	✔
4.	✔	✔	✔	✔

Tool	Example
6. Anecdotal information Incidental information noted mentally, for example, the quality of the questions students ask; contributes to a balanced picture of achievement.	Vivian takes an awfully long time to find what she's looking for in the library. I must ask her what strategies she uses for accessing information.
7. Parent input Information that parents observe in settings outside of school	Joseph had a lot of trouble with that assignment. He said he didn't know where to start.
8. Portfolio A collection of meaningful pieces of information that shows student achievement of processes and products over time; contains relevant information using all of the above strategies for collecting information and can be referred to in order to make data-driven decisions.	When viewing this semester's work samples, self-evaluation sheets, teacher observations, criteria checklists, it's easy to see that Chris has significantly developed his skills in organizing and developing ideas in writing.

Involving the Learner

Adolescents are conceptually sophisticated and are beginning to move towards becoming mature learners. If they are given opportunities to jointly negotiate clear criteria in advance and know what they are supposed to be learning, they don't have to guess what is in the teacher's head. Encourage students to take ownership and control of their learning through self- and peer-assessment activities. Useful tools that involve the learner include self-assessment sheets, marking keys, rubrics, reflective journal writing, portfolio assessment, and peer assessment.

Central to the task of improving assessment is the collection of baseline data, through the use of potent assessment tools (both qualitative and quantitative) that provide a rich source of diagnostic information. Teachers can use these for a variety of purposes. Data collected at the school level provides a snapshot of the range of ability across the school. Data collected in the classroom provides a snapshot of what is happening in every classroom and in every subject area. The analysis of such data identifies strengths and weaknesses and indicates where to put strategies in place to ensure improvement. As problem areas are targeted, further data collection will indicate whether or not these various strategies are working. Ongoing assessment and monitoring processes enable teachers to continue to gather and compare information about the level of students' understandings and about their learning skills, and provides accurate information for evaluation purposes.

CHAPTER 3

Adolescent Learners and Literacy

In the early years and at primary school, there is usually an explicit focus on the teaching of literacy, as there is on the teaching of a range of learning processes. In the middle school, content begins to exert more influence. This is not to deny that many teachers in these year levels continue to teach students how to learn, rather than just what to learn. Nevertheless, the sense of a lot of content to get through begins to emerge in the middle school, before dominating at senior levels.

(Lountain and Dumbleton, 1999, A, p. 25)

At the very time when literacy is required as the key for successful learning, it tends to be overlooked, taken for granted, or relegated to a place of lesser importance. Rather than "assuming knowledge," it is critical that middle and secondary school teachers recognize the diversity of language development of their students and the diversity and language requirements in other subject areas.

Literacy for adolescents means that nothing should be taken for granted. Yet it is often the case in middle and secondary schools that nearly everything related to literacy learning is taken for granted. It cannot be assumed that all students come to high school being able to write and read competently and that they share the same passion for subject matter as their teachers. In the secondary context, they face greater exposure to informational texts and these texts can have readability levels beyond that of many students. It can be quite common to find students working with a specified textbook, even though it might be unsuitable for a number of them.

Literacy Is the Key

Schools have always played a crucial role in determining life opportunities and providing access to language and literacy practices that are considered to be important in society. Those people who have the ability to use language appropriately in a range of contexts and for a variety of purposes, are said to have acquired "cultural capital," which allows them access to a greater number of life choices.

School literacy means being able to engage effectively in the language practices reinforced and valued in the school context. It also means being able to make meaning of school subjects. Language and literacy are linked, and are an integral part of this making and sharing of subject-specific meaning. Teachers and learners use language in the social context of the classroom to make and negotiate meaning, and therefore literacy and language underpins all school learning. Students demonstrate their learning, as well as their command of a number of subject languages, through the literacy skills of listening, speaking, reading, writing, viewing, and critical thinking. Literacy skills are therefore a tool for learning, as well as an indicator of success at school.

Curriculum Standards: Literacy Requirements

Most school systems have established achievement expectations to measure student progress in each learning or subject area. The expectations or outcomes are contained in curriculum framework statements published by provincial education departments. References to literacy are threaded through the descriptions in each of the learning areas. They are often accompanied by statements that literacy skills need to be developed across the curriculum, or assume that the acquisition of literacy skills is inherent in the course.

> *In arts courses, students develop their ability to reason and think critically as well as creatively. They develop their communication and collaborative skills, as well as skills in using different forms of technology.*
>
> (The Ontario Curriculum, Grades 9 and 10: The Arts, 1999, p. 3)

> *Students will need to be able to acquire knowledge, to interpret and communicate information, and to solve problems and make decisions. In doing all of this, students require a wide range of critical and creative thinking skills that they can apply to a variety of situations . . . as self-motivated, self-directed problem solvers and decision makers who are developing the skills necessary for learning.*
>
> (Alberta Learning, Social Studies 10-20-30, 2001)

> *Students in Grade 10 Mathematics will describe issues to be considered when collecting data (e.g., appropriate language, ethics, cost, privacy, cultural sensitivity).*
>
> (Government of British Columbia Ministry of Education, Mathematics Curriculum, 2001)

> *The major aim of the K-12 Science program is to develop scientific literacy in students.*
>
> (Saskatchewan Education (1991), Science K-12 Curriculum)

Literary development has concentrated traditionally on the elementary years of schooling. Whether there are detailed, specific literacy requirements for adolescents or not, what is contained directly or indirectly in prescribed expectations or outcomes statements emphasizes the increasing sophistication required of students in the production and response to texts. Typically, the requirements make reference to the need for adolescent students to be able to

- employ a variety of techniques or strategies
- use technical terms appropriately
- exhibit control over the use of conventions
- choose from a variety of devices to shape text for different audiences
- demonstrate critical awareness of how texts are constructed
- access curriculum literacies

The common theme is for adolescents to progress towards achieving the literacy-related outcomes expected of mature learners.

The Changing Nature of Literacy

Literacy is not static. It can look different across workplaces, homes, and schools because different cultures and contexts require, reinforce, and promote literacies that are valued in their community.

From a Single Literacy to Multiliteracies

Our understandings about what it means to be literate change as society changes. In the past, it was possible to participate effectively in society using only functional literacy skills (such as correct paragraphing, spelling, sentence structure, grammar). These skills are still vitally important today, but effective participation in society today also requires knowledge of how to understand and apply a range of literacies, including critical, creative, technological, visual, cultural, and multi-literacies.

New technologies have rapidly changed our understandings about literacy and the way we use language. Adolescent learners are becoming more proficient at handling, locating, analyzing, extracting, storing, and using increasing amounts of information. They understand and apply a much wider range of literacy skills than their earlier counterparts, for a wider variety of purposes. As new methods of communication emerge, they will continue to develop new ways of accessing, using, and combining information into different types of texts.

In the future, adolescents will have to learn to become readers, writers, and users of new computer-based media and multimedia genres that combine visuals, sound, and words in non-linear patterns with graphics, images, and video.

Technology has had and is having a profound impact on the way teachers and schools operate. In some classrooms, there is already a widening gulf between teachers' and students' experiences with technology. Some teachers feel threatened by the fact that they do not have the same expertise as their students.

As with any tool for learning, students need exposure to, and opportunities to practise using, different technologies. They need to be able to decide whether or not the technology will help them achieve their purpose, whether or not it is appropriate for their needs, and whether or not it will be available at the time when they need it. A key skill of learning is being able to select the most appropriate technology to fulfil a particular task. Initially, it might be useful to suggest two to three options for presenting work, until students are able to make appropriate choices confidently.

It is important to remember that new technologies support learning and teaching. Teachers will be required to learn and teach the different features as well as the ways different technologies can be used, but they will still draw on their pedagogical beliefs to inform their decisions. "Computers must be placed within a sound framework of what we believe education to be and how we believe it should be done" (Spencer, 2000).

Already many students are experienced and confident users of new genres created by new technologies. The notion of a community of learners becomes a reality when students and teachers share and pool their expertise and knowledge.

From Functional to Critical Literacies

It is imperative that students gain mastery over language. They must be able to communicate effectively with others using universally accepted conventions. Functional literacy is therefore not an option. It is non-negotiable. However, as adolescents move towards adulthood, they will need much more than the basic learning tools to enable them to make progress outside school. Today's curriculum has to work, not only in the present but also for the future (Kress, 1996) and therefore teachers and schools cannot concentrate solely on functional literacy. They cannot forget about computer, visual, critical, cultural, and all the other multiliteracies that students are already starting to face now and will increasingly face in the future.

Much of the information that adolescents access from texts, the Internet, and television is unmediated. As students engage with these new forms of literacy, they will also need to be equipped with skills that they can use to analyze the validity and source of information.

Critical literacy approaches recognize that meaning is not fixed in, or by, texts, and that it is possible to have multiple, optional, and contradictory interpretations of the one text. They also recognize that texts, as "versions of reality," carry values associated with power, gender, and race, and that they shape the way in which students construct their world.

It is becoming increasingly important that students know how texts work, how they situate and manipulate readers, and how they position them to read or interpret situations in particular ways. The types of questions students need to ask include:

• Who is the author of this text?

• Why was it written?

• What is its message?

• What version of reality does this present?

• Whose interests are served by this message?

• Whose interests are not served by this message?

• Is anyone likely to be marginalized by this text?

• What are the gaps and silences?

• Does the message reflect my thinking? What is missing? What needs to be added?

Without the tools to carry out this type of critical analysis, students are unable to determine the values that are implicit (or explicit) in texts, and are left vulnerable to manipulation.

There is a fine line, then, in balancing the need to teach the fundamental basics of language (functional literacy), with the need to attend to the other literacies. All of these literacies reflect the reality of the world today — as well as the world of tomorrow.

Designing Support at the School Level

Mastering school literacies means mastering curriculum literacies. In each subject, literacy involves learning to use its specialised language, its distinctive vocabulary, as well as its symbolic, graphic, pictorial and diagrammatic representations. Teachers and learners use language to make and negotiate meaning of subject specific content in the social context of the classroom. Together they use language to read, write and talk about subject specific content. What students read and write about, what they say, and how they say it, is unique to the particular context of the learning area. Literacy is therefore not something added on, or treated separately within a learning area. It is the vehicle for communicating and understanding subject specific content.

(Chapman, 1996, p. 4)

Attending to literacy and mastering subject content are therefore two sides of the same coin. Students need support to be able to understand and effectively use the specific language of different learning areas. When students' literacy skills are improved they process information more effectively, they have greater understandings about subject-specific content, and they improve their learning outcomes.

Establishing a Whole-School Approach Model

A whole-school approach to literacy recognizes the breadth of achievement within the school and demonstrates consistency and continuity in teaching, learning, and assessment practices across all classrooms.

A whole-school *literacy policy* enables all teachers to come to common understandings about literacy, and to articulate a set of values about literacy that all teachers support.

As part of the literacy policy, many schools implement a whole-school *literacy audit.* Teachers collect, collate, and analyze qualitative and quantitative data about students' literacy levels from all learning areas and various sources across the school. They seek out data where gaps in information are detected. Schools may decide to conduct a whole-school testing program to provide baseline information about students' skills.

Debates about issues related to the use of teacher judgments or test results can be avoided if the best aspects of both approaches are implemented. Teacher assessment based on detailed knowledge of the students over time and over a variety of situations clearly have more validity than a one-off test that is probably only partially relevant. But these take time, can be hard to collate, and may lack a common standard.

The ongoing collection and analysis of data highlights areas that need to be addressed. Teachers can be informed of the findings of the whole-school audit and opt for a *whole-school literacy priority* that will be addressed by all teachers, in all learning areas.

Once a literacy priority has been determined, teachers in learning areas need to develop, collaboratively, an action plan that targets the area of need. The plan needs to identify the amount of support that team members need in order to tackle the literacy priority. It also needs to include outcomes, related strategies, resource/role allocations, timelines, and a set of criteria for determining success.

The literacy leader and/or members of the literacy committee have an important role to play in a whole-school approach. They have the expertise to discuss, explain, and model ways in which to incorporate particular literacy strategies within subject-specific content, as well as strategies that will effectively target the whole-school literacy priority. This can be done at the classroom, learning-area, or whole-school level. When teachers share common understandings about students' needs and about the effectiveness of particular literacy and learning strategies, they are able to work together to effect improvement.

The following form shows how, following school-wide discussions about literacy, one school obtained data for its literacy focus.

■ Whole-School Literacy Focus

Students will develop active and attentive listening skills.

Today you will receive (personally or through your Literacy and Learning Committee member) the data collection forms for monitoring listening skills in your classroom.

The form has been divided into the three categories which teachers identified earlier in the term as being of concern:

• Listening for instructions
• Listening manners (individually, in small groups and in the classroom)
• Listening for main ideas (supporting details, translating information)

The process is simple.

Please select two students (one lower ability/one average ability) from your class (student 1 = lower ability, student 2 = average ability).

The form is double-sided (one page per student).

Write the number (i.e. 1 or 2 - see the code above) and the student's name in the space allocated at the top of one of the two pages and complete the other relevant details in the top section of the page.

Reflect on any checklists/anecdotal information of listening behaviour and others that you have collected over the past weeks; in-class observations you have made, outcome levels you might have previously identified, and then read the outcome pointers on the form.

After reflection, please use your professional judgement to indicate the appropriate level achieved by the student for each category.

On the right hand side (in the margin) please write a summary of the student's level for each category (3 levels should be recorded in the margin).

Hand your completed form to your team Literacy and Learning Committee member.

Example of monitoring process

Literacy teachers and/or members of the Literacy Committee are well placed to be able to develop collaboratively a set of criteria that can be used as a monitoring tool for the literacy priority, and to coordinate the collection and analysis of data. The ongoing assessment and monitoring of data indicates when the combined effort of all teachers is making a difference.

Other Models

Teachers are responsible for attending to the learning needs of all students. This is not an easy task when there can be wide gaps of ability within each classroom. It is not practical to attempt to provide a different learning programme for every student in every class, but it is also not beneficial to simply "teach to the middle of the class" and hope for the best.

Teachers can meet the needs of adolescent learners through combinations of whole-class teaching, small-group work and individual teaching. They can introduce new topics, concepts, or skills at the whole-class level, and have individuals or small groups work on activities related to the whole-class activity. The teacher is then available to work with individuals or groups on other necessary skills. At the end of the lesson/topic/program, the whole class can share understandings, reflections, or summaries.

While some students will manage to make progress with their learning with a modicum of assistance, others will need more targeted support. Maintaining consistent, quality support can be difficult in the middle and secondary school context because of frequent changes of teachers and subjects. Despite the best efforts of teachers and schools, a significant number of students continues to fall through the cracks.

The majority of schools provide support at a variety of levels.

The Student Withdrawal Model

Some schools use withdrawal classes. Students at educational risk are withdrawn from class to work individually or within a small group with a support teacher. Research tends not to recommend withdrawal models, because of the "modelling" benefits that occur in the mainstream classroom and because of the negative labeling that is often attached to withdrawal. ESL students, in particular, need to be exposed to constant modelling of the target language.

Withdrawal groups are most effective when they are conducted for short periods of time, for specific purposes, and when learning progress is carefully monitored. There is a danger that gaps in learning will widen if withdrawal activities are unrelated to the regular curriculum, thereby defeating the reason for withdrawal.

> *Let me get this straight — we're behind the rest of the class and we're going to catch up to them by going slower than they are?*
> (Bart Simpson, 1996)

Common sense, however, needs to be applied to each situation. Little is gained if these learners remain in the mainstream classroom and their needs are ignored. Nor is anything gained if they consistently receive little or no explicit literacy instruction across classes. Some students will no doubt pick up literacy skills through osmosis or learn them "on the job." A significant majority, however, will continue to fall through the net.

The aim of any intervention program is to improve learning outcomes. Withdrawal programs are not all ineffective. Gifted and talented students are often withdrawn so that they can work with students who share similar abilities and interests. Students at educational risk also benefit from participating in short-term special projects that enable them to work with their peers, and enhance their self-esteem. There is no joy in continually failing in the mainstream classroom.

Programs that enable students at educational risk to engage in carefully planned, rewarding language experience activities can be extremely beneficial. They need, however, to be short, motivational and targeted. Specific outcomes and a set of criteria should be determined in advance and data needs to be collected at regular intervals, so that progress can be closely monitored. Ongoing, explicit feedback is very important and extremely potent. It helps students understand what they have done well and what they need to do next in order to make further progress. When students can demonstrate that they have achieved the target outcome/s, they can move on.

The Literacy Support/Team Teacher Model

In some schools, students at educational risk move from class to class. A literacy support teacher might occasionally support the mainstream teacher. Variations of team teaching might occur, and the support teacher might take a whole class, small group or individual through aspects of literacy while the regular teacher focuses on the content.

Alternatively, the support teacher might take the class while the regular teacher moves around, teaching at the point of need. They plan the learning program together as a team.

Generally speaking, little explicit teaching of literacy occurs once the support of the literacy teacher is removed, because mainstream teachers may not have the knowledge and training to support students who are encountering difficulty. This means that these students' at-risk status is likely to increase. A worst-case scenario happens when the at-risk student moves across classrooms, with no teacher having the skills to cater to his or her learning needs. Too often, mainstream teachers remain disempowered because they lack the skills or confidence to know what to do.

The English Department Model

Many secondary school support models promote a model of literacy support where one or two literacy or ESL teachers, or members of the English department, take on the responsibility of monitoring literacy across the school. The roles of these teachers are vitally important, because they are able to support other teachers to identify literacy demands and can suggest appropriate strategies. However, it is difficult for one or two people (or several members of one learning area) to be stretched adequately across the school so that every student at educational risk, every ESL or gifted and talented student — or for that matter every teacher needing assistance — gets the help he or she needs. English teachers, like all other teachers, have a large amount of content that they are expected to cover, and it can be unrealistic to add the monumental task of supporting all other teachers with the task of monitoring student literacy in all learning areas.

It is also unrealistic to expect that skills learned in one 40- or 50-minute English period will be automatically transferred to other learning areas, because each learning area uses language differently and for different purposes. A focus in one area of the curriculum does not necessarily support the successful and independent application of literacy skills across all subjects.

When schools rely exclusively on the literacy support teacher or English department model, mainstream classroom teachers also get a very clear message that literacy is something that "others" do; that it is hard; that it is something only "experts" can take on board; that it is not their responsibility to teach literacy; and that literacy is something that can be "fixed" in 50 minutes. They become dependent on other people to improve their students' literacy skills. Many believe that if the literacy support teacher is working with their students then their students' literacy problems are being adequately addressed and there is little else the teachers need to do. With training, though, all teachers can develop the skills required to support students' learning.

The Sharing of Responsibility Model

Students and schools need to work consistently on literacy skills. Intermittent campaigns for literacy improvement tend to be ineffective in the long term. What is needed is a sustained and consistent approach to literacy. Many schools have found that sharing responsibility for literacy among teachers (at the subject-area, grade, or whole-school level) makes the task of literacy improvement much easier. While the work completed in each subject area might be different, common aspects of literacy (spelling/grammar, paragraph writing, written and oral genres, note-making skills, and research processes) can be explicitly taught, reinforced, and monitored by teachers in different learning areas. When teachers work towards common goals for literacy improvement, students' literacy skills tend to improve in all subject areas.

Whole-school or subject-department models for literacy improvement have many benefits. Energy is harnessed in one direction and funding can be put aside for resources linked to improvement. Students get plenty of opportunities to practise, develop, refine, and consolidate their literacy skills in the context of different subject-area content, by the teachers who know the language of their subject better than anyone else. This does not necessarily mean that all teachers need to become literacy teachers. It does mean, though, that they need to become familiar with a wide range of strategies that they can use to help support students as they tackle the literacy demands of the subject area.

The Volunteer, Coach, or Peer Tutor Model

Some schools find volunteer or peer tutor programs to be a beneficial and supportive component of their school literacy improvement strategy. Students' self-esteem is markedly raised because of the nurturing nature of the support and encouragement that they receive during such programs. The aim of the program is negated if volunteers and students do not get along, so care needs to be taken to ensure close matching. All stakeholders benefit when key teachers at the school provide a training program. Volunteers or peer-tutors need to be given a range of short activities that reinforce subject-specific content or that target specific literacy skills. They also need to have opportunities to participate in regular forums where they can discuss issues, share ideas, and receive support.

Focusing on Literacy at the Classroom Level

Mastering a subject means mastering the literacy of the subject. In mathematics, for instance, students are required to comprehend and compose a range of written and oral genres that use mathematical language, tables, graphs, symbols, and formulae. Teachers need to be aware of the demands that these tasks place on students. They also need to teach, model, and/or demonstrate explicitly the specific vocabulary and the language features and structures of genres that are common to their subject area. Students demonstrate their understandings of subject-specific content through language. When students have time to improve ther literacy skills, they are able to demonstrate their understandings more effectively. Improving literacy skills means improving learning outcomes. Attending to literacy and mastering subject-specific content are therefore two sides of the same coin. Literacy is the vehicle for communicating and understanding subject specific content.

When teachers are familiar with a range of strategies, they can put in place those that help students make further progress towards target learning outcomes. Some things can be done in the short term, and at the classroom level, to implement a strategy for improving literacy. The following section outlines the importance of:

Awareness

Planning

Action

Reflection

Awareness

The most crucial thing that teachers can do is to be aware of what adolescent learners face in the middle and secondary school context. This means observing students closely as they work and noting problem areas. It might mean selecting an aspect of literacy (listening, speaking, writing, reading, or critical thinking) and looking closely for literacy demands embedded in related oral, writing, and reading activities, tasks, texts, and practices.

A teacher's day is often so busy that he or she can't plan to "stop to look." It can be interesting to make time to observe what is actually happening — to look more closely, for example, at the quantity and quality of talk that takes place. Who does all the talking? What do they talk about? What opportunities do students get to talk? Is interactive, small-group work encouraged? Are key instructions or key words written on the board to help ESL or ESD students? What happens to spelling errors in students' work? Are they circled by the teacher, and then largely ignored by students? Do students ever get time to go back over two or three assignments, note feedback, and set goals for improvement? Sometimes students don't realize that they repeat the same spelling errors frequently, or that teachers from different subjects have written similar feedback about their work.

It may be useful to reflect on whether students get opportunities to read a portion of text silently before being asked to read it orally. If not, they are sight-reading material. Are they expected to remember lengthy instructions, without having key actions being listed on the board? Are some tasks too difficult for them to master? Would it help if tasks were broken down into smaller, more manageable components?

Without this kind of analysis at the classroom, subject-area, grade, and/or whole-school level, teachers will continue to be oblivious to the literacy demands they place on students. Sometimes informal observations don't provide accurate information about an aspect of literacy or learning. It might be necessary to collect baseline data to identify problem areas. This can be done through the use of survey forms, questionnaires, checklists, retrieval charts, or video recordings.

It is important to be aware that the majority of adolescent learners prefer to fade into the background. They don't relish undue attention, particularly if the fact they are struggling is highlighted. They are particularly resistant to being given work that looks like primary-school work or being treated like grown-up primary school children. They therefore need developmentally appropriate strategies or strategies that have been modified for them. "One size fits all" approaches such as guided or shared reading (where aspects of texts are highlighted and discussed) need to be used with discrimination and in different ways.

Sometimes it is more discreet to offer support at the small-group level, so that individual students do not feel conspicuous.

Planning

Once problem areas have been determined (through observation or analysis of data) and targets for improvement have been set, then careful planning needs to take place to ensure that all students will be able to reach those targets.

If necessary, break tasks down into manageable units. Incoporate opportunities for reinforcing specific literacy skills (such as predicting, visualizing, inferring, note-making, identifying difficult vocabulary) at various points of the learning journey. Build these moments into teaching because literacy skills need to be taught and reinforced many times before they become internalized.

Literacy skills can't be taught once, and then left to chance. If the final outcome of a program of work, for example, involves writing a persuasive argument, the teacher and class need time to discuss the conventions and structure of the genre, and to negotiate a writing framework for the genre. Students will need opportunities to practise, develop, and refine the skills required to write a powerful persuasive argument through ongoing mini-lessons, support, and explicit feedback.

Literacy demands increase in number and in complexity as students move through their schooling. This is another reason why it is important to teach literacy skills in middle school and then continually reinforce them each year. The skills then become tools for learning that students can apply independently. When students know a range of strategies, they can concentrate on the complex concepts and tasks that they have to tackle in secondary school.

Action

Analysis without active response leads nowhere. With targets set, strategies need to be put in place to support movement towards the targets. The correct support strategies are key.

Students, as well as teachers, need to build up their own repertoire of strategies that they can access for various purposes. This means that they need to be given opportunities to learn about the purpose of different strategies, to practise implementing them, and to reflect on their effectiveness. They will become more adept at selecting appropriate strategies for tasks if they are regularly given opportunities to select from a range.

Tackle problem areas by identifying learning goals (or target outcomes) and putting in place strategies such as explicit teaching, coaching, modelling, and explicit feedback to ensure progress toward the goals. Continue to observe students as they work on tasks over a period of time and in a range of contexts. It can be helpful to use a set of criteria, a checklist, or retrieval chart while making observational notes, as a reminder of the focus. This process of monitoring, or keeping a close watch on what is being learned, is an ongoing process and it informs the teaching/learning program. The teacher selects, modifies, or changes strategies accordingly.

Performance improves with practice. Tennis players get better at tennis by practising. Saxophonists play more proficiently when they have plenty of practice. It's the same with language. Students become more proficient users of subject-specific language when they hear it, see it, speak it, and write it. They have to be exposed to it. They have to be able to "approximate" it. And they have to be given opportunities to refine it before they can apply it confidently. Teachers who model ways of using language in informal talk and class discussions, who highlight and explain key words encountered in texts, and who encourage the use of glossaries and journal writing will find that students start to use the language of the subject area naturally, without realizing they are doing so.

Adolescent learners need to be able to practise using language in order to get better at using language. Students use language to demonstrate their understandings. It is important to provide time for them to engage in these processes. (ESL students need to be able to use their first language to internalize new concepts.) They need to be able to think things through, to talk and write (in order to clarify ideas), to explore concepts and to explain their thinking. They need to do these things independently as well as in collaboration with others. As they do so, they enrich and extend their vocabulary, as well as their proficiency with language.

Reflection

Without reflection, learning is likely to plateau or slow down. Reflective thinkers question and assess all aspects of their learning. They identify what they did well, what they might need to do next, and what they might do to improve the learning next time. This type of thinking enables them to be active, independent, and self-directed in their approaches to learning tasks. It prevents them from repeating behaviours and ensures that they make progress with their learning.

As students become more proficient at this type of thinking, they develop higher-level metacognitive or thinking skills that enable them to monitor and regulate their own learning. These skills include elements of analysis, problem solving, and evaluation. Strategies such as journal writing and three-level questions (which probe for evidence, or require inferences to be made) provide opportunities for students to practise using higher level thinking processes. ESL students will use their first or preferred language when reflecting.

Teachers also benefit from engaging in reflective practices. They can reflect on the quality and quantity of students' learning. They can use reflective thinking processes to inform their practice and to determine the effectiveness of particular strategies on students' learning outcomes.

If reflection reveals that students are making little or no progress, then it will be necessary to change tactics. This might mean modifying or changing the learning program, in some cases; many times, until students start to make progress. Other students may need an expanded repertoire of strategies or texts at a different reading level. You may need to teach some skills explicitly, or re-teach them so that students can focus for a longer period of time on a specific skill.

Improving Support for Teachers

The challenge of improving learning for adolescents is emerging as a key issue for schools and school systems. Sustaining improvement is a vexing problem. Many fine schools achieve success consistently, sometimes in the most trying circumstances. It often proves difficult to replicate that progress elsewhere, just as it proves difficult to be sure that students who struggled to learn in the past are finally on the road to continuing success.

There is no easily applied formula or guarantee of an instant solution. Improving learning for adolescents in middle and secondary schools requires a consistent, well-resourced, long-term effort. The key messages emphasized throughout this text, and which seem to form the basis for lasting improvements in learning, can be summarized in a series of seven reminders.

Reminder 1: The Importance of Context

The school context for adolescent learning is special and different. It is important to understand, analyze, and work with the context, and to change those elements that can be changed. Effective leadership and a supportive culture are important ingredients for success.

Reminder 2: Emphasize the Appropriate Learning Principles

Adolescent learners are different. They need to be responded to in ways that reflect those differences. The responses need to be based on learning principles that are

- grounded in research and well tested observation
- powerful enough to sustain lasting, long-term improvement
- linked to practical, "do-able" activities at the school and classroom level

Reminder 3: Focus on Literacy in Learning Areas

Literacy is the key to improving learning in middle and secondary schools. There is a need to move on from the generalized notions of language across the curriculum to

- focus on the demands of the learning-area outcomes
- focus on responding to those demands specifically, explicitly, consistently, and practically

- focus on functional literacy and multiliteracies required for the new millennium

Reminder 4: Use Practical Strategies

Strategies for effective learning in middle and secondary schools incorporate literacy and subject-area emphases. For learning to be purposeful, to slow or stop the secondary achievement dip, teachers can't adopt strategies randomly or carelessly. Strategies need to be selected by

- careful planning based on students' needs (for motivation, challenge, and support that enables them to tackle the literacy demands of learning areas)
- discriminating precisely the match between strategies and the likelihood that they will assist progress towards particular outcomes or objectives (some strategies, for example promote reading; others target writing objectives)

Reminder 5: Work on a Variety of Fronts

Improving learning for adolescent students requires a continuing effort over time in a variety of areas. Individual teachers contribute a lot to the improvement effort. Their task is easier if the organization, culture, and support within the school are synchronized with teachers' goals.

Reminder 6: Expand the Repertoire

Strong pressures have acted in concert to narrow the instructional response to the needs of adolescent learners. To improve learning, the repertoire of responses needs to be expanded to include consideration of a variety of

- school organizational arrangements
- school support models for literacy
- learning, teaching, and assessment strategies

An extended repertoire will enable students to acquire literacy and learning skills within subject content. Improved skills will result in

- more effective processing of information
- greater understanding of subject content
- better learning outcomes

Reminder 7: Provide Ongoing, Explicit Feedback

Adolescent learners, in particular, are very concerned with having a sense of fair play about their learning. They like to receive clear, open, and explicit feedback. When they know what they can do well, what they need to work on next, and what they need to do to improve, they are able to focus their energies in the right direction. Feedback can be provided in a variety of forms, such as one-to-one communication, marking keys and rubrics, anecdotal records, student-teacher interviews, peer-assessment, and teacher or peer response to students' self-reflection.

CHAPTER 5

Learning Strategies

A Teaching Framework for Using Strategies

The Stepping Out framework is an adaption of the ERICA (Effective Reading in Content Areas) reading framework (Morris and Stewart-Dore, 1984). It is an extremely effective model to use when planning a learning program. The framework supports teachers as they

- prepare students before they begin tasks
- provide support strategies that help students think through and organize their ideas during tasks
- determine ways in which students can demonstrate their understandings after completing tasks

Investing time in before and during activities means improved understanding and improved subject-area outcomes.

The Stepping Out framework follows.

Stepping Out Teaching Framework

Before (What will you do to prepare students for the task?)	**Background Information**	*Select strategies that* • activate background knowledge • link existing knowledge to new information • review, extend, enrich, and clarify vocabulary and concepts
	Awareness of Purpose	*Select strategies that* • motivate students' interest • establish a purpose for the activity
During (How will you help students think through and organize ideas?)	**Thinking Through**	*Select strategies that enable students to* • think through ideas • self-monitor their understandings
	Organizing	*Select strategies that help students to* • extract and organize relevant information for a specific task
After (How will you get students to demonstrate or translate their understanding?)	**Using New Information**	*Select strategies that enable students to* • evaluate ideas critically • demonstrate understanding of learning

Planning from the Framework

When planning to teach a learning activity or program:

1. Start at the after stage to determine

- the target learning objectives
- how students can best demonstrate these target learning objectives

2. Move to the before stage to determine

- where students sit in relation to the target objectives/outcomes
- how to bridge the gap between their existing knowledge and knowledge to be learned
- which strategies best facilitate students' understandings and mastery of new vocabulary
- whether there are concepts, skills, or subskills that students need to learn, and how best to teach them
- how to link the learning to authentic contexts

3. Plan the during stage to determine

- the kinds of support strategies that will enable students to think through the activity and to organize their thinking (for example, three-level guides, directed silent reading, retrieval charts)
- the type of assessment that you can integrate into the process

Using the Framework for Planning

1	After (Demonstrating)	**What are the target learning objectives?** What understandings/skills do I want students to demonstrate? How can students best show this?
2	Before (Preparing)	**Where are my students relative to the target learning objectives?** What do they already know? What else do they need to know? What task or strategies will enable them to build on their existing knowledge? What strategies can I use to teach the concepts, skills, or subskills involved in this task/lesson/unit?
3	During (Engaging)	**What key points/concepts will students need to learn?** What support will they need to do this? How can they organize their information? Which strategies would be useful? What type of assessment can integrate into the process (for example, ongoing observational notes, checklists, self-assessment forms)?

Teaching from the Framework

- When using the framework in the classroom, start from the before stage and move through the during and after stage.

- It is not necessary, and it is too time consuming, to plan before, during, and after activities for each and every lesson. Some strategies are best used at the before or during stage of a learning program. Others can be used effectively at any stage of the learning process. Make your choices based on the purpose of the activity and the needs of students.

- Time invested in before and during activities leads to an improvement in the quality of students' leaning outcomes and is time well spent.

- A useful sequence of strategies for a classroom lesson might look like this:

Using the Framework for Teaching

Before **(Prepare students for the** **learning that lies ahead.)**	• Brainstorm ideas, or • Provide an anticipation guide, or • Provide an overview of the unit or lesson
During **(Provide scaffolding so that** **students can think through** **their ideas and organize** **their information effectively.)**	• Jointly devise a retrieval chart, or • Use a framework so that students can record their research information, or • Provide a series of focus questions, or • Ask students to draw a "mind map"
After **(Provide opportunities for** **students to demonstrate their** **understandings.)**	• Produce an oral report, or • Perform a group role-play, or • Write a persuasive argument, or • Report back to the class

eneral Strategies

trategies	Before	During	After	Concept	Skill	Reading	Writing	Listening	Speaking
Briefing the Prime Minister	✔	✔	✔	✔	✔	✔	✔	✔	✔
Card Cluster	✔	✔	✔	✔	✔	✔	✔	✔	✔
Dictogloss		✔	✔	✔	✔	✔	✔	✔	✔
Envoy		✔	✔	✔	✔	✔	✔	✔	✔
Exit Slips		✔	✔	✔	✔	✔	✔	✔	✔
Jigsaw		✔	✔		✔	✔	✔	✔	✔
K-W-L (Knowledge-Wonder-Learned)	✔	✔	✔	✔	✔	✔	✔	✔	✔
Literature Circles	✔	✔	✔	✔	✔	✔	✔	✔	✔
Marking Keys	✔	✔	✔	✔	✔	✔	✔	✔	✔
Modelling	✔	✔	✔		✔		✔	✔	✔
Pros, Cons, and Questions	✔	✔	✔	✔	✔		✔	✔	✔
Quartet Interviews		✔	✔	✔	✔			✔	✔
Rotating Groups or Papers		✔	✔		✔	✔		✔	✔
Rubrics	✔	✔	✔	✔	✔	✔	✔	✔	✔
Small-Group Work	✔	✔	✔	✔	✔	✔	✔	✔	✔
Structured Overview		✔	✔	✔	✔	✔	✔		
SWOT Analysis	✔	✔	✔		✔	✔	✔	✔	✔

Briefing the Prime Minister

1 What is the purpose?

- To analyze, summarize and synthesize information
- To practise note-making skills
- To work collaboratively and cooperatively with a group
- To create a culminating event with a purpose
- To present information succinctly

2 How can I implement the strategy?

1. Identify the purpose for the reading at the beginning of the assignment: Each small group will identify its position on a topic and choose a lobbyist who will have five minutes to brief the prime minister on the position.

2. Divide the class into small groups. Each group identifies its lobbyist as well as its position on the issues.

3. Group members gather their information, synthesize it, and prepare a briefing paper of clear, strong, talking points. They should also make notes of answers to questions they anticipate being asked by the prime minister and his/her aides.

3 What am I looking for?

Observe whether students

- collaborate in group work
- pose higher-order thinking questions
- analyze and synthesize information
- organize and apply information
- understand concepts and content

4 How can I collect information?

METHOD	EXAMPLE
Self-assessment	**Self-assessment** It was a good idea to let Jimmy be the lobbyist since he talks the most. It was hard keeping the presentation to only five minutes — there was a lot to say.
Peer assessment	
Teacher observations	**Teacher observation** The challenge here was to find enough different topics for the groups to present to the prime minister. Next time, I'll make sure that I have sufficient variety so that each group has a different topic to present.
Criteria checklists	
Anecdotal information	
Parent input	
Portfolio	

Card Cluster

1   What is the purpose?

- To collate ideas discussed at the small-group level
- To distinguish between main ideas and supporting detail
- To organize ideas
- To support and develop ideas

2   How can I implement the strategy?

1. Distribute several cards and one marker to each small group.
2. Explain that the purpose of the exercise is to generate and then organize ideas about a topic.
3. Provide clear directions of what is to be recorded.
4. Ensure that key words are recorded clearly on cards.
5. Ask one group member to pin up the group's cards so that related ideas are clustered together.
6. Ask other groups' representatives, one at a time, to cluster their cards. New ideas are placed in a new space, same ideas on top of previously pinned card, and cards related to a pinned card are placed near it. Students may be asked to justify their arrangement of cards.

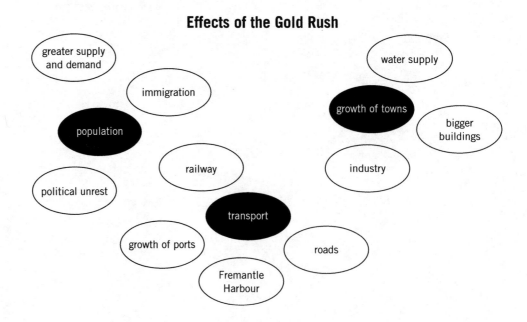

Effects of the Gold Rush

3   What am I looking for?

Observe whether students

- understand content
- generate ideas
- organize information meaningfully
- select key words and phrases
- distinguish between main ideas and supporting detail
- demonstrate metacognition by
  - knowing when to use a card cluster
  - applying the strategy independently
  - applying the strategy to appropriate contexts
  - support and develop ideas

4   How can I collect information?

METHOD	EXAMPLE
Self-assessment	**Teacher observations**
Peer assessment	Anthony can generate ideas but has difficulty seeing the relationships between them.
Teacher observations	**Criteria checklist (small group)**
Data-driven decisions	
Criteria checklists	
Anecdotal information	
Parent input	
Portfolio	

Criteria checklist (small group)

CRITERIA	STUDENTS' NAMES			
Generates ideas				
Distinguishes between main idea and supporting detail				
Organizes information meaningfully				

Self-assessment

At first I couldn't understand why the other groups clustered their ideas in the way they did. But when I listened to their explanations it gradually became clearer. I understand the topic really well now.

Dictogloss

1 What is the purpose?

- To use subject-specific vocabulary and standard correct English
- To extract key information from a text
- To clarify ideas not understood in a text
- To process new information

2 How can I implement the strategy?

1. Explain to students that they are going to listen to or view the text twice to understand its meaning.

2. Read the text aloud to students or have them view the selected portion of video. Ask students to focus on the meaning of the text.

3. Read the text aloud or have students view the video again, this time pausing at appropriate places for students to record key words and phrases.

4. Students work in pairs to compare notes, adding or clarifying information with their partner's help.

5. Each pair joins with another pair to share information. By this stage, the group should have a fairly accurate record of the original text. Determine the level of students' understanding by listening to their discussion.

6. Group members write up their information as a group, in pairs, or individually. Each group reads its final version to the rest of the class.

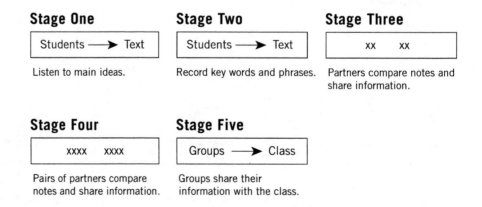

Stage One

Students ——▶ Text

Listen to main ideas.

Stage Two

Students ——▶ Text

Record key words and phrases.

Stage Three

xx   xx

Partners compare notes and share information.

Stage Four

xxxx   xxxx

Pairs of partners compare notes and share information.

Stage Five

Groups ——▶ Class

Groups share their information with the class.

What am I looking for?

Observe whether students

- demonstrate understanding of content
- extract and record the main ideas in a text
- support their interpretation of the text
- ask questions for clarification
- write in standard correct English
- embed subject-specific vocabulary in their work
- distinguish between main idea and supporting detail

How can I collect information?

METHOD	EXAMPLE
Self-assessment	**Self-assessment**
Peer assessment	I had a lot of difficulty understanding the extract the first and second time but I learned a lot by asking my friends questions.
Teacher observations	**Teacher observations**
Data-driven decisions	Mei Lin has written over a page! Her ideas are presented in the appropriate text form and she has developed and supported
Criteria checklists	her ideas. And she has used some vocabulary of the original text. This is a significant step forward. She obviously
Anecdotal information	understands the concepts covered. From the evidence in this piece of work Mei Lin has moved from level 3 to level 4 on the
Parent input	school's literacy continuum.
Portfolio	**Data-driven decisions**
	When I review the information collected on Earl's outcomes over the last few week (his written work, his self-assessment forms, my observations, the information I have noted mentally) it becomes clear that he is generally working at level 4 on the literacy continuum.

Envoy

 1 **What is the purpose?**

- To provide structure and accountability to group discussions
- To learn from each other and take responsibility for learning
- To develop listening and oral skills
- To synthesize and summarize skills

2 **How can I implement the strategy?**

1. Place students into groups and give them a topic for research or discussion.

2. Choose one student from each group to be the envoy who will report to other groups.

3. Each group completes its discussion or research. Each envoy visits another group and reports the research or outlines the discussion. Information might include what ideas or suggestions were made, what conclusions were reached, what decisions were made, and so on.

4. The envoy listens to a report from the group that she/he is visiting.

5. The envoy returns to the original group and shares the information learned from the other group.

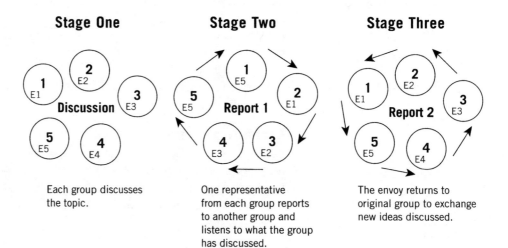

Stage One	Stage Two	Stage Three
Each group discusses the topic.	One representative from each group reports to another group and listens to what the group has discussed.	The envoy returns to original group to exchange new ideas discussed.

3 ## What am I looking for?

Observe whether students

- summarize and synthesize ideas
- organize information clearly
- demonstrate background knowledge
- understand concepts discussed
- listen effectively
- question critically and reflect on ideas

 4 ## How can I collect information?

METHOD	EXAMPLE
Self-assessment Peer assessment Teacher observations Data-driven decisions Criteria checklists Anecdotal information Parent input Portfolio	**Peer assessment** Yasmeen reported on her group's discussion. She explained their ideas clearly. All of us understood what she said because she organized her ideas logically and gave us examples for each idea. **Teacher observations** The students in Taro's group were listening very intently. They synthesized effectively what the envoy said. **Anecdotal information** More opportunities to summarize and synthesize ideas needed. Over half the class had trouble. **Criteria checklist**

Criteria checklist

CRITERIA	STUDENTS' NAMES			
Summarized the main ideas effectively				
Organized ideas in report effectively				
Sound level of understandings				

Exit Slips

1 **What is the purpose?**

- To monitor comprehension and provide a roadmap for future teaching
- To provide informal assessment of the success of a lesson
- To assist with planning, teaching, and re-teaching

2 **How can I implement the strategy?**

1. In the last few minutes of class, ask students to write on an index card or slip of paper a comment about what they read or studied in class.

2. Students can pose a question that they haven't had answered yet, identify the most important idea of the class, predict what will happen next, point out something they found confusing, and so on. Alternatively, ask them to answer a question such as: What is one thing that you have learned today? What do you want to learn more about tomorrow? Do not grade or correct this informal writing.

3. Collect the exit slips. Read them to assess the effectiveness of your teaching and decide where to begin tomorrow. You might want to use some comments anonymously to begin the class the following day.

Exit Slip **Name:** _____

1. What did you learn in this class today?

2. What are you still unsure about?

3. What do you want to learn more about tomorrow?

---

3 **What am I looking for?**

Observe whether students

- understand the material
- synthesize information
- refer directly to the text for understanding
- comment on the effectiveness of a particular strategy or presentation

4 **How can I collect information?**

METHOD	EXAMPLE
Self-assessment	**Self-assessment**
Peer assessment	I learned today that the Bruce Trail runs the entire length of the Niagara Escarpment. Tomorrow, I'd like to know what happens if someone falls and gets hurt on private property that's part of the Bruce Trail.
Teacher observations	
Criteria checklists	
Anecdotal information	**Anecdotal information**
Parent input	From the "best-laid plans" department: I thought I had nailed this lesson. Apparently, there are still many unanswered questions out there. Back to the drawing board.
Portfolio	
Note-checking	

Jigsaw

1 What is the purpose?

- To provide a structure for small group work
- To encourage participative, cooperative learning and place responsibility for learning on the student
- To cover a broad amount of information efficiently

2 How can I implement the strategy?

1. Place students into home groups, for example, six groups of four. Give each student an aspect of a topic to discuss or research such that each student in each group has a different focus.

2. Students from each group form expert groups to study their aspect together. Students research their information in the expert groups and prepare to report to their home group.

3. Students move back to their home groups and report as the expert on their aspect of the topic.

Topic _____

Aspect _____

A. _____   C. _____   E. _____

B. _____   D. _____

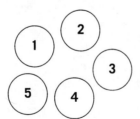

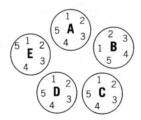

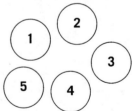

1. Sharing or Home Groups
   Original Group

Stage One

Each group member is allocated a different aspect of a topic.

2. Expert Groups
   Reconstitued Group

Stage Two

Group members reform so that they all have the same respect of the topic about which to become expert.

3. Return to Sharing
   or Home Groups
   Original Group

Stage Three

Students return to their original groups. Each student reports on what they have learned.

3 What am I looking for?

Observe whether students

- demonstrate understanding
- are engaged in the activity
- use subject-specific vocabulary
- critically analyze, evaluate, and apply ideas
- support their ideas
- summarize and synthesize main ideas

4 How can I collect information?

METHOD	EXAMPLE
Self-assessment Peer assessment Teacher observations Data-drive decisions Criteria checklists Anecdotal information Parent input Portfolio	**Self-assessment** I learned a lot about probability through today's jigsaw. I found it really helpful to ask questions of the rest of the group.

Criteria checklist

CRITERIA	STUDENTS' NAMES			
Understands the main ideas				
Displays evidence of subject specific vocabulary embedded in classroom language				
Displays ability to support and develop ideas				

Anecdotal information

Dwayne's English teacher confirmed my judgment that his ability to express himself orally is improving. Today in a jigsaw activity he summarized the group's discussion clearly and succinctly.

K-W-L (Know-Wonder-Learned)

 1 ## What is the purpose?

- To access prior knowledge about a topic
- To make predictions
- To visualize the content of a text
- To link prior knowledge to inquiry
- To provide a research strategy for inquiry

2 ## How can I implement it?

1. Identify a topic.

2. Decide how to record the information in three (or four) columns: K, W, and L; the fourth if you want it is G, for where to go to find the answers. Use chart paper, a reserved area of the board, overhead transparencies, or other means that students can access for ongoing reference. Students work individually or in groups to tell what they know about the topic.

3. Students group, organize, categorize, and label the ideas in the "K" column.

4. Using the "K" column as a starting point, students develop the "W" column: what do they wonder about? What do they want to know about the categories in "K"?

5. Connect the wondering questions to the categories in the "K" column.

Know	Wonder	Learned
• Beothuk lived in Nfld • First Nations • extinct	• How long had they lived there before Europeans? • What were their interactions with Europeans? • How did they become extinct? • Why didn't anyone do anything to help them stay alive?	

6. If you wish, complete the "G" column. Where will students go to find out the answers to questions in the "W" column?

7. Apply newly learned information to the "L" column: what students have learned about the topic. Groups or the whole class can do this as the information is revealed.

3   What am I looking for?

Observe whether students

- collaborate in group settings
- link prior knowledge to new information
- pose higher-order thinking questions
- synthesize and analyze information
- organize and group information into meaningful categories

4   How can I collect information?

METHOD	EXAMPLE
Self-assessment	**Self-assessment**
Peer assessment	Who knew that *Shakespeare in Love* wasn't a true story? I thought that the movie was based on the play (*Romeo and Juliet*).
Teacher observations	
Criteria checklists	**Teacher observations**
Anecdotal information	General knowledge in this class is good. The challenge will be finding new sources of information for them.
Parent input	
Portfolio	

Literature Circles

1 What is the purpose?

- To ensure participation and engagement in reading
- To model the steps that good readers take when they read: question, inquire, connect, focus, visualize, apply
- To encourage collaborative work that is purposeful and meaningful

2 How can I implement the strategy?

1. Model the strategy using cooperative volunteers and brief pieces of text (newspaper articles, one-page magazine essays, and so on).

2. Establish norms of behaviour for the strategy as a whole class:

   - take turns speaking
   - disagree constructively
   - listen with intent — make eye contact with the speaker, lean in, nod, confirm
   - comment on others' ideas
   - be tolerant
   - stay focused
   - come prepared
   - act responsibly in your group

3. Limit groups to five or six students, each with a specific role to play. Allow 40 to 50 minutes for the activity, and remind students to use their other during-reading strategies: note-making skills, self-stick notes, it says/I say, and others, as preparation for the literature circle. Role sheets may be helpful as students learn the process, or as reminders during the year.

4. Here are some typical roles that students will play in the literature circle (Daniels, 1994). Modify the roles based on the needs of your class.

   The *Questioner* creates questions to lead the conversation in the literature circle: What were you wondering about as you were reading this material? Why were certain examples used? Why were things described in a particular way? What was the writer's perspective or point of view? What questions did you have when you were finished this article or section? What were one or two of the most important ideas presented?

   The *Connector* finds connections between the reading material and the world outside; draws connections to her personal life, happenings in school or the community, historical situations, or to other people or problems that come to mind.

   The *Passage Master* locates key sentences or paragraphs to which he thinks the rest of the group should pay attention: parts that were important, puzzling, interesting, thought-provoking, surprising, or confusing, and then reads the passages aloud to comment on, explain, or discuss them.

The *Vocabulary Enricher* presents words that the other members of the group will need to notice and understand, provides dictionary definitions, and tries to identify the words' meanings in context.

The *Illustrator* draws a picture (cartoon, stick drawing, diagram, flow chart, timeline, or other image) related to the reading, and asks her group to speculate what it shows; at the end, the illustrator explains what the picture means, what ideas prompted it, or what it represents.

The *Researcher* finds some background information about the topic to present to the group, including artifacts (books, Web sites, maps, drawings, paintings, models) that will help the group to understand the material better.

5. The teacher is the observer, facilitator, and assistant. Circulate, but only interrupt a literature circle if the group is struggling or seriously off task. If you do join a group, you are there as a group member, not the leader. If the group does need help, offer a question and then move on immediately.

3 What am I looking for?

Observe whether students

- work collaboratively
- defend ideas with evidence from the reading
- visualize
- develop higher-order questions
- connect to other subjects, works, and personal experiences
- recall information
- analyze and synthesize information

4 How can I collect information?

METHOD	EXAMPLE
Self-assessment Peer assessment Teacher observations Criteria checklists Anecdotal information Parent input Portfolio Note-checking	**Note-checking** Students place all of their role sheet notes and self-stick notes in a portfolio. You collect these as a written record of students' work in their literature circles. **Teacher observations** The students in Rina's group enjoy one another's company — lots of laughing but they appear to be on task.

Marking Keys

1 What is the purpose?

- To provide a clear indicator of expectations for a piece of work
- To indicate the scoring method for students' work
- To provide explicit feedback

2 How can I implement the strategy?

1. List the skills involved in a task. Include aspects such as use of subject-specific words, working well with others, neatness, and presentation. List the skills that students need to complete the task, and then provide a rating scale (5-1) for their abilities to successfully apply the skill. If "neatness" is a criterion for legibility or understanding, what skills will students need to apply to score a 5?

2. Alternatively, construct a marking key with students. Students can attach the marking key to their work when they hand it in.

3. Consider having students use marking keys as self-assessment sheets. Students can compare their results to yours.

page 155

3 What am I looking for?

Observe whether students

- adhere to the marking key criteria
- use the marking key to inform their work

4 How can I collect information?

METHOD	EXAMPLE
Teacher observations	**Self-assessment**
Self-assessment	At last I know exactly what's in my teacher's head. I know I need to spend more time on my paragraph writing, because the mark allocated for that section is high by comparison with the rest.
Peer assessment	
Data-driven decisions	
Criteria checklists	**Teacher observations**
Portfolio	Everyone in the class seemed happy with the marking key. The "rules" were made clear before they began and they felt they were a fair way of marking.

Modelling

1 What is the purpose?

- To make explicit the cognitive processes and skills that learners use when they complete a task

2 How can I implement the strategy?

1. Choose a process or strategy with which you are comfortable, such as extracting key words or phrases, brainstorming, or guessing the meaning of a word in context.

2. While the class watches, 'think aloud' the steps of the process you are following. Record your work on the board or on an overhead.

3. Encourage students to become familiar with the process by having them model skills for one another.

Peers and teachers can try modelling some of these skills

Steps for completing a homework task	How to set out direct speech
How to access particular information in the library	How to conduct a writers' conference
How to solve a problem	How to combine simple sentences
How to construct a paragraph	How to use a journal for different purposes
How to ask for clarification	How to complete a concept map (or other diagram)
How to listen effectively	
How to read maps, graphs	How to decide when to use a table of contents and/or an index
How to write in a particular text form	How to develop and support ideas
How to generate a note-making framework	How to select an appropriate text form
How to work cooperatively with other students	How to skim a chapter
How to edit	How to resolve conflict at the small group level
How to write an effective topic sentence/paragraph	How to generate ideas for writing
How to set out references in a bibliography	How to study for a test

3 What am I looking for?

Observe whether students

- apply the appropriate vocabulary
- articulate what they are thinking, visualizing, predicting, connecting

4 How can I collect information?

METHOD	EXAMPLE
Teacher observations Self-assessment Peer assessment Data-driven decisions Criteria checklists Portfolio	**Self-assessment** When I talk through how I'm going to read a map, I have to think about what the map language is — this is more difficult than I thought because I usually do this automatically without saying it out loud. **Teacher observations** Forcing students to articulate their thought processes has shown that some students take poorly thought-out shortcuts or jump to conclusions that have landed them in trouble.

Pros, Cons, and Questions

1 ## What is the purpose?

- To provide a framework for exploring an issue
- To consider different points of view

2 ## How can I implement the strategy?

1. Explain the purpose of the activity.

2. Explain the meanings of headings *Pros* and *Cons*. Point out that what one group sees as a pro may be viewed as a con by another group.

3. Students in pairs or small groups list as many ideas as they can in the time provided. They generate and record questions.

4. Students present an oral report of their ideas or cluster the cards they created.

5. Discuss student-generated questions at the whole-class level.

6. Students can use the *Pros, Cons, and Questions* chart as a framework for their writing.

■ **Pros, Cons, and Questions**

Issue: _____

Pros	Cons

Questions: _____

page 157

3   What am I looking for?

Observe whether students

- understand the issues associated with a topic
- consider others' points of view
- analyze an issue critically
- demonstrate metacognition by
  - explaining the value of the strategy
  - applying the strategy independently to appropriate contexts

4   How can I collect information?

METHOD	EXAMPLE
Self-assessment Peer assessment Teacher observations Data-driven decisions Criteria checklists Anecdotal information Parent input Portfolio	**Teacher observations** Ellis, Karl, and Tuan worked really well using their *Pros, Cons, and Questions* chart. They were able to consider different points of view. They knew about the issues. **Anecdotal information** In Health Education the teacher tells me Nicole suggested using a *Pros and Cons* chart to explore an issue in her Health Education class. She showed him the strategy which worked very well. **Parent input** You know how hard Gabriel finds it to organize his ideas and keep focused? Well, that *Pros and Cons* Chart you set for homework worked really well. He gained a real sense of satisfaction from finishing a piece of work.

Quartet Interviews

1 What is the purpose?

- To work in a group to get information about a given topic
- To practise language skills
- To develop cooperative learning skills
- To develop active listening skills

2 How can I implement the strategy?

1. In groups of four, group member 1 interviews group member 2. At the same time, group member 3 interviews group member 4. Partners switch roles. The group reassembles, and students share their partner's response. If necessary, model an interview to the whole group.

Stage One   Group members work together to develop a set of questions related to a topic.

Stage Two

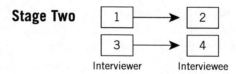

Interviewer   Interviewee

Stage Three

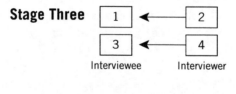

Interviewee   Interviewer

Stage Four

1 & 2 ← 3 & 4

Pairs share responses

2. As you begin using this strategy, set the questions yourself or brainstorm ideas for questions with the whole class or a number of groups.

3. As students become more familiar with the strategy, they can generate their own questions at the small group level and begin to manage the strategy independently.

4. Alternatively, students work in groups of three, incorporating a reporting or recording role.

3 What am I looking for?

Observe whether students

- demonstrate background knowledge
- listen effectively and actively
- summarize and synthesize ideas
- develop rigorous questions
- support and develop their ideas
- express understandings in their own words
- work cooperatively

4 How can I collect information?

METHOD	EXAMPLE
Self-assessment	**Self-assessment**
Peer assessment	After interviewing Maurice and listening to what he knew and thought about terrorist attacks, I realized that I had to work out what my opinion and thoughts were — and not just repeat what others said. It really made me think "What do I know? How do I feel about this?"
Teacher observations	
Data-driven decisions	
Criteria checklists	**Criteria checklist**
Anecdotal information	
Parent input	
Portfolio	

CRITERIA	STUDENTS' NAMES			
Sound level of background knowledge				
Clearly justifies opinions held				
Values the ideas and opinions of others				

Rotating Groups or Papers

1 **What is the purpose?**

- To cover several topics efficiently
- To promote student-centred, collaborative problem solving
- To provide opportunities for revision of concepts
- To encourage critical thinking

Topic: Social Problems in Urban Areas

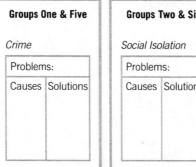
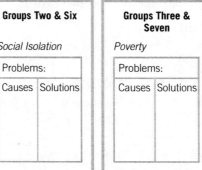

Groups One & Five	Groups Two & Six	Groups Three & Seven	Groups Four & Eight
Crime	*Social Isolation*	*Poverty*	*Housing*
Problems:	Problems:	Problems:	Problems:
Causes / Solutions	Causes / Solutions	Causes / Solutions	Causes / Solutions

2 **How can I implement the strategy?**

1. Assign each group an issue or aspect of a topic. Groups record their ideas on chart paper.

2. After a set amount of time each group rotates clockwise to the next sheet of paper. One student stays behind to talk through the issues/ideas recorded. The group at the next sheet of paper considers the ideas recorded and then adds any new ideas. If there is no reporter, the visiting group can use check marks to show ideas they think are effective and add question marks to ideas that need clarification. After about two minutes, the groups rotate in the same direction to the next sheet of paper and repeat the activity.

3. Depending on the purpose of the activity the groups may not need to rotate through all stations. Where students have recorded question marks, a discussion at the whole-group level may be necessary.

4. Use this strategy on its own or as preparation for a follow-up activity.

3 **What am I looking for?**

Observe whether students

- demonstrate understandings
- think critically
- identify key issues
- support and develop their ideas
- work collaboratively

4 **How can I collect information?**

METHOD	EXAMPLE

Self-assessment

Peer assessment

Teacher observations

Data-driven decisions

Criteria checklists

Anecdotal information

Parent input

Portfolio

Peer assessment

Group Two's chart showed they had really understood the causes and solutions of housing problems. They had several clearly explained reasons. Their chart helped me to better understand the issue.

Criteria checklist

CRITERIA	STUDENTS' NAMES			
	Tom	Jo	Tuan	Bryn
Displayed sound understanding of the issues				
Developed and supported ideas				
Organized his/her talk clearly and logically				

Rubrics

1 ## What is the purpose?

- To identify expectations for an assignment
- To identify assessment criteria
- To provide explicit feedback
- To self-assess while working

2 ## How can I implement the strategy?

1. Begin an assignment by negotiating the marking rubric with students.
2. Students re-state the assignment, including its purpose and expectations. They brainstorm a list of criteria to look for in the final product.
3. Organize the list into broad categories (content, presentation, style, grammar and accuracy, meeting deadlines, and so on.)
4. Decide together on the value of each category out of a total of 100 points.
5. For each category, students identify how to earn the total number of points, as well as the other point levels within the category.
6. Reproduce the rubric on a single sheet for student reference.
7. Students use the rubric for self-assessment as they work. They can also use it for peer-assessment during the course of the assignment.

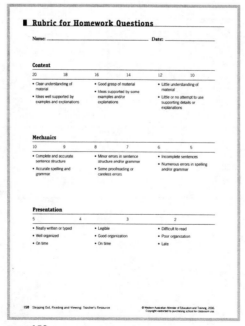

page 158

③ What am I looking for?

Observe whether students

- adhere to the assessment criteria
- self-assess as they work
- apply the skills necessary to meet the criteria

④ How can I collect information?

METHOD	EXAMPLE
Self-assessment Peer assessment Teacher observations Criteria checklists Anecdotal information Parent input Portfolio Note-checking	**Peer assessment** You have many good points in this paper. Content is excellent. Appearance needs some work — I had trouble reading parts of it. You are missing a title page. Are you going to include a map to get the full points for presentation? **Anecdotal information** When students use the rubric to prepare their assignments, the assessment results are usually quite good. By having a target and knowing how to hit it, most of them can rise to the challenge. On this assignment, they've done an excellent job with the content, and the presentation and style marks are continually improving.

Small-Group Work

1 ## What is the purpose?

- To learn through language
- To clarify and extend ideas
- To practise language skills
- To embed subject-specific vocabulary
- To create opportunities for peer teaching
- To develop cooperative learning skills

2 ## How can I implement the strategy?

1. Explain the purpose of the activity and give clear directions and a time limit for the task.

2. Divide the class into groups.

3. Each group appoints a timekeeper, a leader, and a recorder.

4. Remind students that they are accountable for their work which may include reporting back to the whole group, reporting to another group, and completing written work.

5. Monitor the groups to see if they are staying on task. Is the group maintaining focus? Does the group need more time?

6. Involve students in evaluating their cooperative learning skills.

page 159

3 What am I looking for?

Observe whether students

- understand concepts and content
- use subject-specific vocabulary
- work cooperatively
- think critically
- synthesize information
- apply their understandings to other contexts

4 How can I collect information?

METHOD	EXAMPLE
Self-assessment	**Self-assessment**
Peer assessment	I worked quite well in my small group today. I kept to the topic and asked lots of good questions. What I need to work on is remembering not to dominate the discussion and to invite quieter members to give their opinions.
Teacher observations	
Data-driven decisions	**Data-driven decisions**
Criteria checklists	Ella is learning to think far more critically now and is prepared to express her ideas at the small-group level. Earlier in the year, she wasn't comfortable giving her ideas.
Anecdotal information	
Parent input	**Criteria Checklist**
Portfolio	

Criteria Checklist

CRITERIA	STUDENTS' NAMES			
Shows sound understanding of concepts				
Shows ability to apply understanding to different concepts				
Shows sound ability to synthesize ideas				

Structured Overview

1 What is the purpose?

- To provide an organizational framework to use to navigate written and visual texts
- To organize ideas for writing
- To distinguish between main ideas and supporting detail
- To recognize relationships between concepts
- To provide a framework for revising main ideas

2 How can I implement the strategy?

1. Develop the main headings and subheadings that give an overview of the relevant topic.

2. Students work in pairs or groups and select key words and phrases, from the text or from their reading and research, that belong with each subheading.

3. This strategy helps students comprehend their learning. Over time, encourage students to develop their own structured overview of a topic.

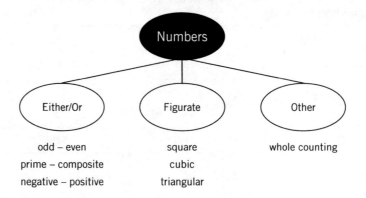

What am I looking for?

Observe whether students

- distinguish between main ideas and supporting detail
- organize their ideas in a meaningful way
- substantiate their ideas by referring closely to the text
- understand the subject content/concepts
- think through their ideas
- demonstrate metacognition by:
  – knowing when to use a structured overview
  – applying the strategy independently to other appropriate contexts

 How can I collect information?

METHOD	EXAMPLE
Self-assessment	**Teacher observations**
Peer assessment	Kylie's structured overview indicates she doesn't have a clear sense of the main ideas we've covered in this topic. It was just a mish-mash of some of the major and minor things we covered. I will need to put strategies in place to focus her on the key ideas of each lesson.
Teacher observations	
Data-driven decisions	
Criteria checklists	**Parent input**
Anecdotal information	That sheet that Jin Ki had to complete was a great idea. Normally he doesn't know where to start when he has to make notes, but the structured sheet focused him on exactly what he had to. He felt very pleased with himself when he had finished it.
Parent input	
Portfolio	

SWOT Analysis

What is the purpose?

- To think from a variety of perspectives
- To discuss different viewpoints
- To focus discussion

How can I implement the strategy?

1. Divide the class into groups of four. With your current topic in mind, assign a viewpoint (strengths, weaknesses, opportunities, threats) to each group member or group.

2. Students read and/or discuss the topic from their assigned viewpoint and take notes as they work.

3. Groups share their work with the class.

■ SWOT Analysis	
Strengths What are the strengths of the text?	**Weaknesses** What are the limitations of the text?
Opportunities What are other potential applications?	**Threats** What risks are involved?

160   Stepping Out, Reading and Viewing: Teacher's Resource   © Western Australian Minister of Education and Training, 2006.
Copyright restricted to purchasing school for classroom use.

page 160

(3)

What am I looking for?

Observe whether students

- extend, develop, and support their ideas
- work cooperatively
- accept other perspectives about a topic
- discuss their own ideas and listen attentively to the ideas of others, even if they have different viewpoints

(4)

How can I collect information?

METHOD	EXAMPLE
Self-assessment Peer assessment Teacher observations Data-driven decisions Criteria checklists Anecdotal information Parent input Portfolio	**Peer assessment** Kamala made lots of good points about the different opportunities she could think of from the reading that we did. Most of the group agreed that it was hard to think about what the threats were, but Lawrence still was able to come up with two or three. **Teacher observations** I need to spend some time explicitly teaching and modelling how to consider 'threats' in relation to the SWOT analysis. A large number of students work with it in the same manner as weaknesses.

Reading Strategies

Strategies	Before	During	After	Concept	Skill
Activating Prior Knowledge	✔			✔	✔
Develop Questions	✔	✔	✔	✔	✔
Diagramming		✔	✔	✔	✔
Directed Silent Reading	✔	✔	✔		
Glossary	✔	✔	✔		✔
Graphic Outline	✔	✔	✔	✔	✔
It Says/I Say/And So		✔		✔	✔
Making Inferences	✔	✔		✔	✔
Note-making Frameworks	✔	✔	✔	✔	✔
Placemat		✔	✔	✔	
Previewing a Text	✔	✔			✔
Reading for Levels of Comprehension	✔	✔	✔		
Re-reading		✔	✔	✔	✔
Say Something		✔		✔	✔
Scavenger Hunt	✔				✔
Self-Stick Notes		✔	✔	✔	✔
Setting Purposes for Reading	✔	✔	✔	✔	✔
Skimming and Scanning	✔	✔			✔
Summarizing			✔	✔	✔

Strategies	Before	During	After	Concept	Skill
Text Reconstruction			✔	✔	✔
Think-Aloud	✔	✔	✔	✔	✔
Think Sheet	✔	✔	✔	✔	✔
Three Levels of Comprehension	✔	✔	✔	✔	✔
Vocabulary in Context	✔	✔			✔

Activating Prior Knowledge

 What is the purpose?

- To support comprehension
- To provide a context for reading
- To activate personal or school-related connections to the reading
- To visualize what the reading will be about
- To stimulate questions about the text
- To make inferences and predictions
- To self-monitor during reading

 How can I implement it?

1. Set the purposes for reading
   - Let students know why this reading assignment is important.
   - Explain how they will use it both immediately and in the future.
   - Let them know what to look for as they read.

2. Activate students' prior knowledge
   - Invite students to brainstorm ideas; create mind-maps; begin K-W-L lists; connect the topics to other experiences, reading, content areas in school; and so on.

3. Develop questions by considering:
   - What do students want to know about this topic?
   - What do you want the students to learn?
   - What elements in the reading should students look for?
   - Establish the facts: who, what, when, where, how.
   - What is the main idea?
   - How might this information connect to what students have read before in this class or others?
   - How might this information compare to other characters, theories, models, stories, heroes, events?

4. Make predictions by asking:
   - What do you think will happen to the hero in this chapter?
   - What do you need to learn from this reading to help us solve the problem?
   - How will learning about this aspect influence your understanding of the broader topic?
   - What are the next steps going to be?
   - How will you (or the main character) be able to use the information contained in this reading?

What am I looking for?

Observe whether students

- are familiar with the topic and terminology
- connect the topic to other subject areas
- predict events, next steps, outcomes
- engage with the topic

 How can I collect information?

METHOD	EXAMPLE
Self-assessment	**Peer assessment**
Peer assessment	Starting with the K-W-L list helped us because we didn't know we knew so much about Columbus.
Teacher observations	**Teacher observations**
Criteria checklists	Thea and Asim worked well on the K-W-L once they realized that they should think about movies and former history classes to generate some ideas.
Anecdotal information	
Parent input	
Portfolio	

Develop Questions

1 What is the purpose?

- To use Bloom's taxonomy to guide development of questions at different levels of difficulty
- To support students' comprehension through the development of higher-order questioning
- To encourage thinking that is deeper than surface-level knowledge

2 How can I implement the strategy?

1. Use Bloom's taxonomy (six levels of thinking: knowledge (recall), understanding, application, analysis, synthesis, evaluation) as a guide to designing questions at different levels of difficulty to meet the learning needs of individual students. You can create the questions or you can work with the students to create them.

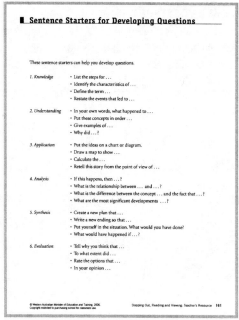

page 161

3   What am I looking for?

Observe whether students

- move beyond factual recall to deeper levels of meaning
- self-monitor reading comprehension based on the questions that they pose
- support their work with direct reference to the text
- synthesize and analyze information
- create and apply higher-order questions

4   How can I collect information?

METHOD	EXAMPLE
Self-assessment Peer assessment Teacher observations Criteria checklists Anecdotal information Parent input Portfolio	**Teacher observations** Louise and Nadia were able to dig into the content here to come up with some good questions — I found myself going back to the text to confirm that my assumptions were correct. Good work. **Parent input** When Jamal showed me the questions that he had come up with for *Fast Food Nation*, I was impressed with the fact that he had related the ideas to his own fast-food experience but wondered how his group would answer his questions.

Diagramming

 1 ## What is the purpose?

- To use the structure of the text to aid comprehension
- To extract and organize important information from a text
- To ensure active meaning-making by thinking through understandings
- To create an organized and structured summary of a text

2 ## How can I implement the strategy?

1. Introduce various diagrams one at a time.
2. Construct a simple diagram on the board with the whole class, or ask students in small groups to complete one that has already been started.
3. After some practice, pairs or small groups construct and compare diagrams.
4. Eventually, students construct their own diagrams independently to suit the particular structure of a text.
5. Alternatively, provide students with a diagram and have them construct a written text that explains the content of the diagram.

Flow Chart

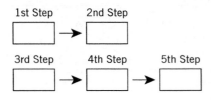

Structured Overview

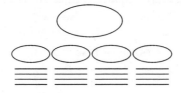

Graphic Outline

| Main Heading |
| Subheading |
| Sub-subheading |
| Sub-subheading |
| Subheading |
| Diagram |
| Caption |

Timeline

4 B.C.E.   1200 C.E.

Hierarchy

Cycle

3 What am I looking for?

Observe whether students

- extract and record main ideas from a text
- organize information effectively
- distinguish between the main ideas and supporting detail
- understand the structure of the text
- demonstration metacognition by:
  - knowing when it is useful to diagram
  - applying the strategy of diagramming independently to appropriate contexts

4 How can I collect information?

METHOD	EXAMPLE
Self-assessment	**Self-assessment** Drawing a flow chart made me realize I don't have to read every word. I learned to skim for the main idea and skip irrelevant parts.
Peer assessment	
Teacher observations	**Teacher observations** Craig has really taken off with diagramming. He now generates his own diagrams independently when note-making.
Data-driven decisions	
Criteria checklists	**Teacher observations** Ingrid's structured overview is completed thoroughly. I can see immediately not only does she have sound understandings of the topic but can organize information effectively and support her ideas.
Anecdotal information	
Parent input	**Parent input** Talia found that structured overview really helpful. She completed her homework in no time.
Portfolio	

Directed Silent Reading

1 What is the purpose?

- To model the reading behaviours used by efficient readers to:
  - promote reading as a problem-solving activity
  - set a purpose for reading
  - encourage students to construct their own questions
  - encourage students to substantiate their readings of the text
  - show students how to guess the meanings of words using context clues
  - promote the critical reading of texts

2 How can I implement the strategy?

1. Students preview a text and predict what concepts it will cover. Set an open-ended focus question as students read.

2. Assist students with their word comprehension strategies through a "think-aloud" example.

3. Students read the text silently and apply word comprehension strategies where necessary.

4. Students write questions for clarification.

5. In small groups, students help each other to answer their questions by referring to the text and discussing the focus questions.

6. Observe and monitor student responses.

7. Discuss unresolved questions at the whole-class level.

3 What am I looking for?

Observe whether students

- use background knowledge and predict content
- use context clues to guess meanings of words
- generate questions of clarification
- understand the main ideas and concepts
- refer to the text to support an interpretation
- read texts critically

4 How can I collect information?

METHOD	EXAMPLE
Self-assessment Peer assessment Teacher observations Data-driven decisions Criteria checklists Anecdotal information Parent input Portfolio	**Data-driven decisions** I observed David and Farha during DSR. They were guessing words in context, generating their own questions, and referring closely to the text to support their opinions. My observations would confirm judgments made in other contexts over the semester, that both of them have a variety of meaning-making strategies when confronted with demanding texts.

Criteria checklist

CRITERIA	STUDENTS' NAMES			
Understands the main ideas				
Supports own reading of text				
Feels confident to construct own questions				

Anecdotal information

As I moved around the classroom I realized that Mal and Sue were having trouble understanding the part about "half lives." When I intervened at the small group level, I realized how weak Mal and Sue's background knowledge is and that I had assumed knowledge they didn't have.

Glossary

 ## What is the purpose?

- To support comprehension
- To build vocabulary and draw attention to particular terms
- To practice inference-making using context clues
- To provide a self-monitoring strategy

 ## How can I implement the strategy?

1. Students create a three-column chart with columns labelled Word, My Understanding, and Defintion.

2. Students identify reasons for selecting particular words, such as words that
   - are unknown to the reader
   - appear to be significant in the context
   - are used in a new or unusual way
   - all have the same grammatical value
   - are particularly effective in the passage
   - are strange or confusing in context

Glossary

Word	My Understanding	Definition
Inflammatory	Intending to antagonize	Tending to arouse excitement, anger
Conservative	Do not like change	Inclined to preserve the order of things
Exposure	To be revealed	To have been laid open to criticism
Racism	To treat people with a different nationality in an unfair way	The belief that other races have distinctive characteristics which determine their respective cultures
Prejudice	A judgment given when all the facts aren't known	A judgment or opinion formed before the facts are known
Bigotry	Attitudes or beliefs which express intolerance	Attitudes, beliefs or actions characteristic of a bigot, intolerance
Denigrate	To regard a character to have little value	Belittle or disparage character of
Discriminate	To act on behalf of prejudice	To act towards someone with partiality or prejudice
Exploit	To use someone unfairly for your own advantage	To use mainly to one's own gain or advantage

3. Model for students how to use the strategy. Identify five or six words from a selection and record them in the Word column. Use the think-aloud strategy to complete the My Understanding column by trying to deduce meaning from context, make connections, make inferences, visualize and so on. Use a dictionary to find an appropriate definition of the word and record it in the Definition column.

4. Students practise using the strategy.

 ## 3 What am I looking for?

Observe whether students

- use a variety of strategies to figure out new words
- determine which words are critical to meaning
- group words by word families, Latin or Greek roots, context clues
- make meaning by using inferences
- recognize the relationship between vocabulary knowledge and comprehension

 ## 4 How can I collect information?

METHOD	EXAMPLE
Self-assessment Peer assessment Teacher observations Anecdotal information Parent input Portfolio Note-checking	**Peer assessment** Jamie needed to look up a lot of words in this chapter. He couldn't figure out the meanings from their use in the book. He slowed us down. **Teacher observation** More time may need to be devoted to some of the terms in this chapter as students seem to be struggling with their meanings and application.

Graphic Outline

1   **What is the purpose?**

- To use the structure of a text to improve comprehension
- To find tools to review or study a chapter

2   **How can I implement the strategy?**

1. Share the purposes for graphic outlines with the class.
2. Provide the class with a completed graphic outline based on an important part of your course text that uses subheadings, figures, and so on.
3. Students either individually or in pairs refer to the text's headings, sub-headings, pictures, diagrams, and so on to complete the graphic outline.
4. When introducing graphic outlines ask pairs to reflect on the value of the activity and its applications.
5. Gradually remove some of the support until eventually students can create graphic outlines independently.

Energy Alternatives Graphic Outline

Instructions: Preview the chapter. Record the name, author, and publisher of the text. Use the heading, subheadings, and figures to fill out the outline.

Chapter 14

| Heading |
| Paragraph 1 |
| Paragraph 2 |
| Paragraph 3 |

Figure 1

| Subheading 1 |

Figure 2

| Subheading 2 |

Paragraphs

| Subheading 3 |

Figure 3

Figure 4

| Summary |
| Concluding Paragraph |

3 What am I looking for?

Observe whether students

- can skim a text quickly and extract the main headings
- predict the main ideas the text covers
- determine quickly the organization of ideas in a text
- demonstrate metacognition by:
  – explaining when it is useful to apply the strategy of graphic outlines
  – applying the strategy independently to appropriate contexts

4 How can I collect information?

METHOD	EXAMPLE
Self-assessment	**Self-assessment** I can see how this strategy will be useful every time I open a non-fiction text.
Peer assessment	**Peer assessment** We want to know how come we haven't been taught about graphic outlines before. All of us were able to work out quickly what the text is about.
Teacher observations	**Teacher observations** Steve and Halina's slow completion of the graphic outline showed that they think it is necessary to read every word of a text. I need to model again how to skim texts and use graphic outlines to determine the main ideas to be covered.
Data-driven decisions	
Criteria checklists	
Anecdotal information	
Parent input	
Portfolio	

It Says/I Say/And So

 What is the purpose?

- To support inference-making
- To make the inferential process explicit
- To provide a method for checking that interpretations are based on information in the text

 How can I implement the strategy?

1. Students create three columns in their notebook or journal: "It says," "I say," "And so."

2. Model the strategy a few times. On the overhead projector or board, create the three columns. Use a sample text and pose three or four questions that will require students to go beyond the facts and to make inferences and draw conclusions. Read a portion of text and then record in the first column exactly what the text says — a sentence or phrase.

   In the second column, using context clues, connections, and predictions, speculate on what the sentence means. In the third column, draw a logical conclusion based on the quotation and speculation from columns one and two.

   For example, using the prologue from *Romeo and Juliet*:

It says	I say	And so
Two households, both alike in dignity/In fair Verona, where we lay our scene/From ancient grudge break to new mutiny.	It means that two families who are well known in Verona and known to each other have some sort of long-standing animosity, and something is going to happen to make it flare up again.	The play will probably be about a disagreement between the two families. I wonder if it means just the immediate families, or their friends and servants (their households) and distant relatives too? And "mutiny" sounds as if there's a group on at least one side who will disobey orders.

3   What am I looking for?

Observe whether students

- make predictions
- make meaningful inferences
- use context clues to read strategically
- determine what words are critical to meaning

4   How can I collect information?

METHOD	EXAMPLE
Self-assessment Peer assessment Teacher observations Anecdotal information Parent input Portfolio Note-checking	**Teacher observations** Jorge is good at using obvious context clues to try to figure out what the text might mean. If I ask him to think of a synonym for a word, he can think of one pretty quickly. That shows his vocabulary skills are improving. **Parent input** As I watched Tonya struggle last night with this exercise, I could see that she just didn't understand the words and didn't seem to have a clue about what to do next. She can decode the words OK but she doesn't know what they mean and looking them up doesn't seem to help!

Making Inferences

1 ## What is the purpose?

- To support comprehension
- To provide skills to jump from disconnected facts to logical meanings
- To demonstrate the thinking processes that independent readers use
- To provide strategies for figuring out meaning from context

2 ## How can I implement the strategy?

1. Model

   An inference is the act of deducing meaning by connecting information in the text with previous knowledge to make an educated guess. Demonstrate inference-making to the whole class or as a mini-lesson for a few students. Think aloud as you
   - stop to question what specific words refer to
   - think about where a certain name has appeared before
   - wonder what a particular word might mean in this context
   - connect an event or a phrase to something that happened before
   - read a sentence or a series of words with different intonation to see if the meaning changes
   - remember facts as they occur and relate them to each other

2. Offer guiding questions

   Provide guiding questions to which students refer as they read:
   - Can you identify all the terms and references?
   - What are the facts that you know so far?
   - What are the explanations for the events to this point?
   - How much do you know about this topic? Can you connect it to other information that you have learned from the text?
   - Why would the writer include this information at this time?
   - Look at a particular sentence. What would be different if the writer had used a different word or phrase in that sentence?
   - Are there words in the passage that you don't understand? Can you figure out their meaning from the context?
   - Are there words or phrases that indicate a point of view that the author is taking?

3. Practise making inferences

Bumper stickers are common external texts that belie an internal text. Invite students to identify the inferences in these bumper stickers. Then ask them to give the 'and so' conclusions that follow.

| BEAT RUSH HOUR: LEAVE WORK AT NOON. |

| HONK IF YOU LOVE PEACE AND QUIET |

| Consciousness: that annoying time between naps. |

| Ambivalent? *Well, yes and no.* |

| Always remember you're unique, just like everyone else. |

3 What am I looking for?

Observe whether students

- visualize events, situations, contexts
- connect information to previous academic or personal knowledge
- question the text and wonder about possibilities
- evaluate information
- analyze information, noticing technical aspects such as language, vocabulary, theme

4 How can I collect information?

METHOD	EXAMPLE
Self-assessment	**Self-assessment**
Peer assessment	I couldn't figure out what was going on from the little paragraph that we had to read in class. I didn't know any of
Teacher observations	the things that other people were talking about.
Criteria checklists	
Anecdotal information	**Anecdotal information**
	Clearly some students are really out of the picture when it comes to photosynthesis. I thought that they had learned
Parent input	something about this before. I'll have to re-think my approach
Portfolio	to this.

Note-making Frameworks

1 What is the purpose?

- To scaffold ways to structure notes effectively
- To organize information from a reading passage
- To understand how main ideas are developed and supported

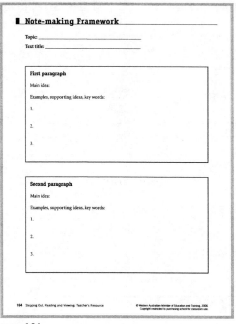

page 164

2 How can I implement the strategy?

1. Provide students with a prepared or class-constructed outline to facilitate note-taking.

2. Identify the topic and reading passage.

3. Model how to identify the main idea of a paragraph and record it in the note. The main idea is usually in the first sentence of a paragraph and will be summarized or reinforced in the last sentence. Remind students that most non-fiction paragraph writing will follow this pattern:
Statement
Elaboration ("In other words…" "That is…" "This means that…")
Examples
Summary

4. Use point-form to record supporting ideas and examples or key words and phrases.

5. Students work in pairs to compare what they have found in the text.

3   What am I looking for?

Observe whether students

- understand subject concepts and to what degree
- identify main idea, key points, and supporting information
- transfer note-making skills to their own expository writing
- demonstrate metacognition by applying the strategy when useful

4   How can I collect information?

METHOD	EXAMPLE
Self-assessment	**Self-assessment** I had a very clear idea of what I had to do. The note-making framework helped me to organize the ideas that I had to take from the book.
Peer assessment	
Teacher observations	
Anecdotal information	**Anecdotal information** This note-making idea is easiest in grade 8 classes if I start with newspaper articles which are quite straightforward in their organization. Then, I'll move on to the social studies textbook.
Parent input	
Portfolio	
Note-checking	

Placemat

1 What is the purpose?

- To promote consensus development
- To learn from one another and take responsibility for learning
- To synthesize and summarize ideas

2 How can I implement the strategy?

1. Students form groups of four.

2. Each group gets a sheet of chart paper and draws a large circle in the centre. The groups divide the outside section such that each student has a work area (see diagram). Students will write their group summary in the circle at the end of the activity.

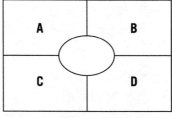

Seating plan

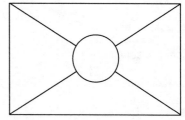

Paper markings

3. Allocate a topic to each group — either the same one to each group or different topics to each group.

4. Students record their individual ideas in their own space on the sheet.

5. After a set time (2-5 minutes), each group member (starting at A) shares his or her work with the others in the group. If any other member has the same point, he or she crosses it out and Person A highlights it. Students continue sharing in order, following the same process until all group members have shared their ideas. The group writes a summary of all highlighted comments in the centre circle of the sheet.

6. Summarize the findings orally or by cutting out and posting the circle from each sheet.

What am I looking for?

Observe whether students

- demonstrate understanding of content
- think critically
- use background knowledge
- listen effectively
- synthesize ideas
- work collaboratively

How can I collect information?

METHOD	EXAMPLE
Self-assessment	**Self-assessment** To start with I wasn't sure that I understood the topic, but then I just made myself write down what was in my head. Hearing other people's ideas made me realize I was on the right track and had thought of some bits that other people in the group missed.
Peer assessment	
Teacher observations	
Data-driven decisions	
Criteria checklists	**Teacher observations** I need to be mindful of selecting who will start the sharing back process. By the time it got to Tori, her two points had already been made by the others in the group.
Anecdotal information	
Parent input	
Portfolio	

Previewing a Text

1 What is the purpose?

- To highlight the structure and organization of a text (see Scavenger Hunt, page 134)
- To use the features of the text to aid comprehension
- To skim and scan a text to locate and extract information and determine relevance (see Skimming and Scanning, page 140)

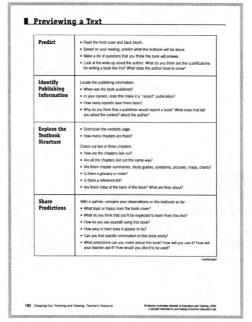

page 162

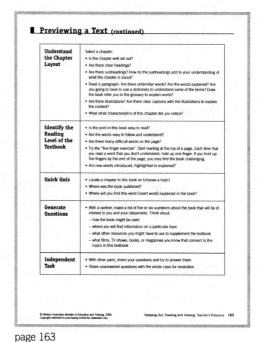

page 163

2 How can I implement the strategy?

1. Use the strategy when introducing a textbook or other form of reading: a journal, a magazine, a pamphlet, a newspaper, a resource kit, and so on.

2. Students view the front cover and blurb of the text and predict what features they might find in the text, including titles, subheadings, introductory and concluding paragraphs, illustrations, captions, and so on.

3. Students preview the text silently for a few minutes looking for its main topics.

4. Partners briefly share their predictions of the main topics.

5. Students write down a question they expect the text to answer.

6. A few volunteers share their predictions and questions with the class.

3 **What am I looking for?**

Observe whether students

- can predict the main ideas of a text
- are willing to take risks in predicting the main ideas
- synthesize the main ideas skimmed in the pre-reading
- understand how the text is organized
- demonstrate metacognition by:
  - explaining when it is useful to apply the strategy of previewing
  - applying the strategy independently to appropriate contexts

4 **How can I collect information?**

METHOD	EXAMPLE
Self-assessment	**Self-assessment**
Peer assessment	Previewing helps me understand the text. It helps show how the ideas are organized and what ideas are covered. I use it whenever I read an informational text.
Teacher observations	
Data-driven decisions	**Peer assessment**
Criteria checklists	Rosa knew about the main ideas in the chapter. She could also explain how the ideas were organized. She was really quick.
Anecdotal information	
Parent input	**Anecdotal information**
Portfolio	Duncan finds it difficult to skim texts. He seems to want to read every word.

Reading for Levels of Comprehension

1 **What is the purpose?**

- To be aware that there are different ways to comprehend text

2 **How can I implement the strategy?**

1. As students read, introduce the idea that there are different levels of understanding the text. In sequence, explain each level: literal, inferential, and evaluative. You might want to use the chart on this page as a guide.

2. Ensure that, on a regular basis, you expose students to the different levels of comprehension. You might do this by having them answer questions at different levels, construct questions at different levels, and classify questions as being literal, inferential, or evaluative.

Level	Definition	Example (from 'The Three Little Pigs')
Literal	An understanding of what is explicitly stated in a text	What did each little pig use to build his house? Who was trying to catch the little pigs?
Inferential	Going beyond an author's literal statements to draw inferences	Why are pigs afraid of wolves? Why did the third little pig build a brick house?
Evaluative	Making a judgment or interpretation of a text	Is it a good idea to build three separate houses? Why? Do you think this is a true story? Why?
Applied/Creative	Going beyond the text to • apply information to new situations • make generalizations • gain additional insights • seek out or express new ideas • respond emotionally	Who do you think might feel sorry for the wolf? Would you rather be a wolf or a pig? Why?

3   What am I looking for?

Observe whether students

- Identify and differentiate among the levels of comprehension:
  - think critically
  - understand the concepts covered
  - refer closely to the text to substantiate their interpretations
  - develop and support their ideas

4   How can I collect information?

METHOD	EXAMPLE
Self-assessment	**Teacher observations**
Peer assessment	Tan finds it difficult to draw inferences and evaluate ideas. I think I will get him to work with Hang, whose comprehension skills are very strong. I'll need to reinforce three-level guides to develop Tan's comprehension skills.
Teacher observations	
Data-driven decisions	
Criteria checklists	**Criteria checklist**
Anecdotal information	
Parent input	
Portfolio	

Criteria checklist

CRITERIA	STUDENTS' NAMES			
Understands main concepts				
Makes close references to the text				
Displays evidence of higher levels of comprehension				

Re-reading

1 What is the purpose?

- To reinforce comprehension
- To make visible the process that good readers use
- To clarify meanings and support vocabulary development

2 How can I implement the strategy?

1. Model the process of re-reading through the think-aloud strategy. Quickly read a passage of text posted on an overhead projector or chart paper. Re-read the passage slowly to demonstrate what good readers do by looping back to an earlier word or sentence, pausing, reflecting aloud, checking the meaning of a word (It Says/I Say/And So, or the Glossary strategy), predicting, and asking questions.

2. Students brainstorm a list of reasons for re-reading. For example, you can re-read when:
   - you can't remember the last word you read
   - there is a graph or a diagram that seems to be important
   - you don't understand a word and need to look it up
   - you are looking for information and you have to refer to the questions
   - you have been distracted by something and weren't paying attention to what you were reading
   - you're not understanding what you're reading
   - you come to a part that was really good and you want to remember it
   - you are confused about a name or character or event
   - a prediction you made has not turned out as you expected.

3. Demonstrate the differences between re-reading for meaning versus skimming a text to find a fact.

Example

In 55 BCE (BCE means Before the Common Era so this is over 2000 years ago), Julius Caesar (This is the same Julius Caesar that we talked about in English and studied in ancient history) led his army into England. They landed in Kent (I need to get out a map and figure out where Kent is) and kept moving northwest until they reached the Thames River (how do you pronounce that word – do you say TH-aims or is it T-ems?) at what is now Southwark (I need to find out where Southwark is too). Aside from a few tribesmen (in England?) on the opposite bank, there was no major settlement. But there was a small port and trading company there (Where? Southwark?) by the time of the next Roman Invasion, 88 years later.

What am I looking for?

Observe whether students

- extract meaning from a text
- apply reading strategies to understand text
- learn increasingly difficult strategies to aid comprehension
- use punctuation to support fluent reading
- use vocabulary retrieval strategies

 How can I collect information?

METHOD	EXAMPLE
Self-assessment	**Self-assessment**
Peer assessment	When I read textbooks, I have to re-read some paragraphs to remember what's going on. I wish I could use a highlighter to mark the words.
Teacher observations	
Criteria checklists	**Teacher observations**
Anecdotal information	Wayne is finally beginning to use some of the strategies that we've been talking about in class. Listening to him read today, he paused at a couple of words, then went back to the beginning of the paragraph to re-read it slowly and I could see him thinking about the meaning of the words in context. His reading is still not fluent or automatic, but he's working at it.
Parent input	
Portfolio	
Note-checking	

Say Something

1 What is the purpose?

- To reinforce comprehension
- To think about content
- To encourage direct references to the text for meaning and intent

2 How can I implement the strategy?

1. Students work in pairs or groups of three. They take turns reading aloud and stop at agreed-upon points: the bottom of the page, after every fourth paragraph, the top of the second column, and so on. At the break, one of the people not reading aloud comments on what was just read. The speaker does at least one of the following:
   - makes a prediction ("I bet that. . .")
   - poses a question for information ("Do you think that. . .?")
   - suggests a clarification ("What this means is. . .")
   - comments on the content ("I liked it when the writer said. . .")
   - connects the content to something else ("This reminds me of. . .")

2. After the conversation, another member of the group reads the next section and stops at the designated "say something" break.

3. The group repeats the process.

Predictions	Questions	Clarifications	Comments	Connections
• I bet that	• Why is	• This makes sense because	• I like the part where	• This reminds me of
• I wonder	• Who is	• This must mean that	• I don't understand	• This part is similar to
• The next thing that will happen is	• What does this mean?	• What they're saying here is	• The best part so far is	• What's different here is
• Because this happened, then this will happen next	• How does this fit with what went before?	• What they said before makes sense now because	• The hard thing about this is	• This event makes me think of
	• Where did we see this earlier?		• I think that	

(3) What am I looking for?

Observe whether students

- make meaningful and relevant inferences
- predict next steps and ask questions
- visualize events and characters
- make connections to other works, subjects, or personal experiences

(4) How can I collect information?

METHOD	EXAMPLE
Self-assessment	**Teacher observation**
Peer assessment	Ken, Sharma and Joe are asking some good questions when they pause, although Joe seems to be having trouble thinking about what might come next.
Teacher observations	
Criteria checklists	**Anecdotal information**
Anecdotal information	"Say Something" lets me see where the needy students are in this class. At the breaks, some students — like Leah and
Parent input	Marco — have difficulty thinking about what to say, even with the prompts on the board. I'm going to have to work with them
Portfolio	to shore up their comprehension strategies.
Note-checking	

Scavenger Hunt

1 What is the purpose?

- To introduce a new textbook
- To become familiar with the layout and content of a textbook
- To analyze the language and terminology of a textbook
- To build vocabulary and draw attention to particular terms
- To practise inference-making using context clues and predictions

2 How can I implement the strategy?

1. Students work in pairs to respond to the list of questions. You might add other questions based on the content area or the text.

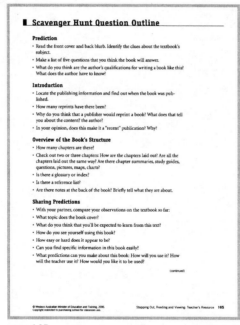

page 165

page 166

2. Give one copy of the book to each student or pair. Have students search for and locate each item on the list. Model the strategy by beginning with the first question on prediction.

3 What am I looking for?

Observe whether students

- work collaboratively to solve problems and find answers
- use a variety of strategies to analyze the book
- make predictions and draw inferences
- pose meaningful questions
- recognize the relationship between visual and written literacy

4 How can I collect information?

METHOD	EXAMPLE
Self-assessment	**Peer assessment**
Peer assessment	Rashad spent a lot of time looking at the pictures, especially the cartoons. We predicted that there was no way that we would ever get through this whole book this year. The best news is that at least it's a new book — published this year.
Teacher observations	
Anecdotal information	**Teacher observations**
Parent input	The students made some good observations about the textbook. They realized that it had some entertaining parts to it but that there were many words that they didn't understand or even recognize. The book's glossary is not that helpful.
Portfolio	
Note-checking	

Self-Stick Notes

1 What is the purpose?

- To locate important information
- To record questions, monitor comprehension, and identify important points
- To begin a note-taking process

2 How can I implement the strategy?

1. Provide self-stick notes that are large enough for students to record questions, comments, predictions, or new ideas.
2. Students use different-coloured notes to categorize responses or note-taking points.
3. Students record on the notes any key points, questions that arise, confusing sentences or concepts, surprising turns of events, or steps in a process. Students keep the notes and refer to them during discussions, assignments, or other related work.

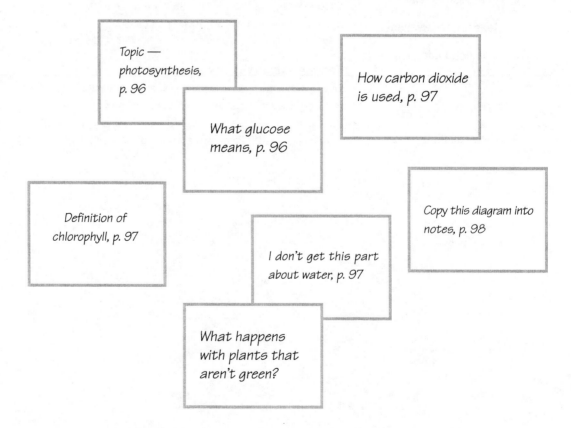

3 What am I looking for?

Observe whether students

- develop higher-order questions
- monitor their own comprehension
- practise comprehension strategies
- synthesize and analyze information
- make connections to other works or personal experiences

4 How can I collect information?

METHOD	EXAMPLE
Self-assessment Peer assessment Teacher observations Anecdotal information Parent input Portfolio Note-checking	**Teacher observations** Lian's book is a sea of coloured self-stick notes. She has organized all her points with different colours which should make it easy for her to write the report later. **Portfolio** Students add page numbers or paragraph numbers to their self-stick notes as they go through the text. At the end of the unit, they stick them on a piece of paper (in order) and include them in their portfolios as evidence of their note-taking work about the text.

Setting Purposes for Reading

 What is the purpose?

- To provide an overview for unit planning
- To give a purposeful structure for the use of before/during/after strategies and culminating events
- To design assignments in manageable chunks
- To ensure that reading and assignments are challenging yet achievable
- To give clear feedback at regular intervals

 How can I implement the strategy?

1. Select reading materials in which students can engage actively.
2. Break the reading assignment into manageable steps or sections so that both short-term and long-term objectives are clear.
3. Provide clear instructions for what students need to achieve or what they're looking for at each step.
4. Set a purpose for the reading by asking students to *do* something with what they'll discover or learn about.
5. Set clear goals, such as discovering plot clues or predicting outcomes.
6. Provide a reason and outcome for the reading such as an oral report, a re-enactment, a map, a jigsaw sharing of information, or the background for a project.

Example

Chapter 5: Upper Canada (pages 46–70)

Review with students what they've learned about Upper Canada so far.

Tell them that they are now looking for details about how Canadian pioneers managed to survive.

At the end of this chapter, students will design and make a survival guide for Canadian pioneers (pamphlet, poster, videotape, and so on).

Break the chapter into chunks and have students work in pairs to read the first three pages using the "Say Something" strategy.

When they've finished, have them go back and use the note-making strategy for these four pages.

What information did they find that they can use in their survival guide?

Students report their findings to the whole class.

---

3 What am I looking for?

Observe whether students

- are reading and at what level
- show comprehension of the text
- use subject-specific vocabulary
- stay focused and on task
- follow through and complete assignments
- summarize and synthesize information

4 How can I collect information?

METHOD	EXAMPLE
Self-assessment	**Self-assessment**
Peer assessment	It's easier for me to read when I know why I have to read this. I like having shorter bits to read rather than long, boring things.
Teacher observations	
Criteria checklists	**Anecdotal information**
Anecdotal information	The boys in this class seem to like the shorter, hands-on assignments. Planning reading assignments that give them something concrete to do with the work really helps them to stay focused.
Parent input	
Portfolio	

Skimming and Scanning

1   What is the purpose?

- To read differently for different purposes
- To gain a general impression of the main ideas of a text *(skimming)*
- To find a specific detail in the text quickly *(scanning)*

2   How can I implement the strategy?

1. Use the words *skim* and *scan* regularly and model when they are appropriate strategies. Provide different opportunities for students to skim and scan.

Skim to

- find appropriate material for an assignment
- review materials to recall main ideas
- skim for a general overview of the topic

Scan to

- find the relevant pages through the table of contents and the index
- find a definition or a specific answer
- re-read information to substantiate an opinion

How to Skim a Text

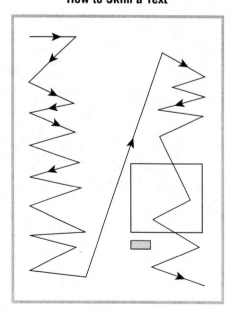

How to Scan a Text

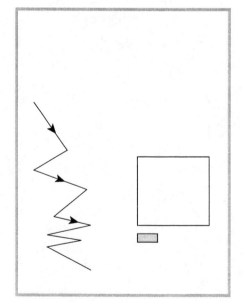

3   What am I looking for?

Observe whether students

- understand how to read for different purposes
- scan for particular information
- skim or preview to gain an overview of the text
- locate information efficiently

4   How can I collect information?

METHOD	EXAMPLE
Self-assessment Peer assessment Teacher observations Data-driven decisions Criteria checklists Anecdotal information Parent input Portfolio	**Peer assessment** Bree was able, after skimming the chapter in one minute, to tell me about the main ideas in the chapter. **Anecdotal information** Cleon takes ages to find particular words in the text when he's completing an Interesting Words chart. I must help him learn to scan the page. **Parent input** Vivien does not know how to find her way around her science book. She takes ages to find the answer to the question. She doesn't seem to know how to use the table of contents and the index nor does she know how to skim a chapter. And she won't let me explain because she says the teacher doesn't do it like I suggest.

Summarizing

 1   ## What is the purpose?

- To think through the ideas in a text
- To distinguish between main ideas and supporting detail
- To translate understandings without copying sections of text

2   ## How can I implement the strategy?

1. Model at the whole class level how to select key words and phrases and record your work on a sheet like the one below. Think aloud to justify your selection. Begin with a short, simple text.

2. Look for opportunities for peer modelling and learning through talk by allowing students to work in pairs to practise selecting key words and phrases. Encourage students to justify their choices to one another.

3. Begin by providing the subheadings. With practice, students will be able to generate their own. It can be helpful for some students to work through the piece of text, crossing out all unnecessary words, phrases, and sentences. When only a few choices are left, the key words and phrases are easier to identify.

■ **Summary Sheet** _____

Topic/Heading: _____

Note-making	Summarizing	
Sub-headings	Key words and phrases	In my own words–subheadings and paragraphs

Stepping Out, Reading and Viewing: Teacher's Resource   **167**

page 167

What am I looking for?

Observe whether students

- understand the subject concepts
- distinguish between the main idea and supporting detail
- justify their selection of key words and phrases
- understand that reading is an active meaning-making activity
- use their notes to translate their understandings in their own words
- analyze critically what they read
- synthesize ideas when more than one reference is used

 ## How can I collect information?

METHOD	EXAMPLE
Self-assessment Peer assessment Teacher observations Data-driven decisions Criteria checklists Anecdotal information Parent input Portfolio	**Peer assessment** Julie was my partner for the notemaking exercise. She kept choosing different key words and phrases from the ones I chose. When I asked her to explain why she thought her words were the key words/phrases, she couldn't tell me. **Teacher observations** Julie's note-making sheet indicates she has trouble distinguishing between the main ideas and supporting details. This confirms her peer's assessment and my observation of the difficulty she has in substantiating at the small-group level. **Parent input** Anil had a lot of trouble making notes for his science assignment on energy. He said the answers to the questions weren't in the book and I must admit even though my skimming skills are pretty good I couldn't find them either. What should Anil have done?

Text Reconstruction

1 What is the purpose?

- To promote active meaning-making
- To make explicit the strategies effective readers use
- To provide feedback about students' comprehension skills

2 How can I implement the strategy?

1. Select a text of less than one page in length the first time you use the strategy, and longer in length once students are familiar with the strategy.

2. Photocopy sufficient copies so that each pair or group has a copy.

3. Cut each text into about five sections. Where you cut the text and how many sections are created will depend on the reading skills of your students.

4. Place the sections of text in envelopes and distribute an envelope to each group.

5. Students reconstruct the text so that it makes sense.

6. Students justify their decisions at the small-group level and, where appropriate, at the whole-class level.

3 · What am I looking for?

Observe whether students

- demonstrate a range of meaning-making strategies (prediction, checking, problem-solving)
- work cooperatively
- identify the main ideas and supporting detail
- demonstrate comprehension
- substantiate their ideas
- listen effectively

4 · How can I collect information?

METHOD	EXAMPLE
Self-assessment Peer assessment Teacher observations Data-driven decisions Criteria checklists Anecdotal information Parent input Portfolio	**Anecdotal information** I watched Melita and Mirsada trying to reconstruct a text which summarized the ideas of the lesson. They weren't able to sequence the events in the gold rushes. It made me realize that they probably hadn't understood what I had said. **Criteria checklist**

Criteria checklist

CRITERIA	STUDENTS' NAMES			
Displays a range of meaning-making strategies				
Refers closely to text to substantiate interpretation				
Listens effectively to other group members				

Think-Aloud

① What is the purpose?

- To articulate thoughts during reading, including images, connections, questions, predictions, and challenges
- To promote metacognitive practice in reading
- To provide a vocabulary and structure on which to build

② How can I implement the strategy?

1. Model the think-aloud for the class, possibly several times, so that students understand the ideas and the language that they should be using.

2. Let students know before you begin that you will be stopping frequently to say what you are thinking.

3. As you read, stop frequently to talk about what is happening in the text and the questions, images, or predictions that you have.

4. When you stop to think aloud, give the students a cue that you've stopped reading and are now thinking.

5. Occasionally, write your comments on an overhead or on the board and ask the students to decide whether you were predicting, visualizing, clarifying, noting confusing details, and so on.

6. After you have modelled the process several times, have students try it in pairs with a portion of the text. Give them sample cues or questions to which they may want to refer. Post these so that students can refer to them and have a comment or question at hand (see the list below).

page 168

7. Encourage think-alouds in the classroom.

8. Offer the possibility of silent think-alouds, where students record their thoughts on self-stick notes. They can use the notes as the basis for talking or writing about the text.

9. Invite students to reflect on how this strategy changed their reading habits.

What am I looking for?

Observe whether students

- articulate what they are thinking, visualizing, predicting, connecting, questioning
- self-monitor their reading for comprehension
- apply vocabulary strategies
- retrieve words automatically
- identify what makes a text difficult and use strategies to eliminate confusion
- use punctuation as a guide to understanding and expression

How can I collect information?

METHOD	EXAMPLE
Self-assessment	**Self-assessment**
Peer assessment	When I follow the prompts on the board to help me with the think-aloud, it's much easier than trying to do it on my own. I find it hard to come up with pictures when we read here.
Teacher observations	
Anecdotal information	**Teacher observations**
Parent input	MaryAnn glosses over any word that is new to her. She can decode it but doesn't appear to worry about knowing the meaning of it once she figures out how to say it. She just keeps on going; she doesn't use word parts or context to figure out what it means. She's still a very dependent reader. She'd like me to tell her the meaning so she can get on with the reading but she's not learning any comprehension skills.
Portfolio	
Note-checking	

Think Sheet

1 **What is the purpose?**

- To develop prediction and substantiation skills
- To make guesses in a safe environment
- To access prior knowledge
- To interact with the text

2 **How can I implement the strategy?**

1. Select a text (for example, a specific section or chapter of a textbook).

2. Decide what are the key concepts in the text.

3. Construct about three topic questions or statements about the key concepts.

4. Create a Think Sheet that includes:
   - the topic questions or statements
   - space for students' predictions
   - space for students to substantiate their prediction

5. Model at the whole-class level how to complete the Think Sheet until students understand the reasons for its use.

6. Give each pair or group a copy of the think sheet. Students work together to complete the sheet. They make predictions, revise if necessary, and record details from the text that support their predictions.

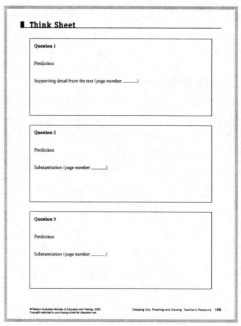

page 169

3   What am I looking for?

Observe whether students

- take risks
- access background knowledge
- refer closely to the text to substantiate ideas
- learn cooperatively
- think critically

4   How can I collect information?

METHOD	EXAMPLE
Self-assessment Peer assessment Teacher observations Data-driven decisions Criteria checklists Anecdotal information Parent input Portfolio	**Teacher observations** Janette and Jenny are usually quiet and aren't prepared to talk in front of the whole class but the Think Sheet got them talking. They worked in pairs, which allowed them to take risks and learn through talking without having to perform. I was impressed by the way they referred closely to the text to support their prediction. Their talk and their writing on the Think Sheet showed they had sound understandings of the subject content.

Three Levels of Comprehension

1 What is the purpose?

- To read texts critically
- To reflect on texts
- To refer closely to the text to substantiate an interpretation
- To develop three levels of comprehension: literal, inferential, evaluative

2 How can I implement the strategy?

1. If using a Three-Level Guide, determine the key concepts or objectives you want students to take from the text. If using Three Levels of Questions, select a range of questions that reflect literal, inferential, or evaluative thinking.

2. Construct several correct and/or incorrect statements for each level of comprehension. Write the evaluative/applied statements first as these give direction and purpose to the guide.

3. Students read the text silently and either complete the Three-Level Guide by writing True or False next to each statement or answer the Three Levels of Questions.

4. In pairs or small groups students compare their responses. Where there is disagreement, students refer closely to the text in order to support their interpretation.

5. Raise with the whole class any issues that can not be resolved at the small-group level.

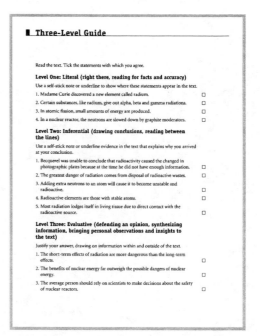

page 170

3   What am I looking for?

Observe whether students

- comprehend texts at different levels
- substantiate their interpretation of the text by referring closely to the text
- think critically and to what degree
- cooperate effectively
- develop and support their ideas
- understand concepts
- consider the ideas of others

4   How can I collect information?

METHOD	EXAMPLE
Self-assessment	**Self-assessment**
Peer assessment	Our group really enjoyed doing a Three-Level Guide. I thought I knew the right answer but when we had to justify our interpretations, I realized it was possible to read the extract in different ways.
Teacher observations	
Data-driven decisions	**Peer assessment**
Criteria checklists	The best part of our group's work was the way we stayed on task. We justified our opinions but we need to learn to listen more effectively to each other. We all wanted to have our own say at the same time.
Anecdotal information	
Parent input	
Portfolio	

Vocabulary in Context

1 What is the purpose?

- To use words and ideas in context to infer meaning

2 How can I implement the strategy?

1. Select useful, unfamiliar vocabulary from a text that students need to read.

2. List on the Vocabulary in Context sheet the selected vocabulary and the page numbers on which the words appear.

3. Model how to
   - skim to locate the words
   - read around the unfamiliar words to find context clues

4. Pairs of students record clues they find in the text. From the clues they explain the term in their own words.

5. Pairs discuss their predictions and answers. Listen to individuals and groups to determine which words you may need to teach and which students may need more practice with this skill.

■ Vocabulary in Context

Read around difficult words in order to infer meaning.

Word/phrase	Page number	What clues to meaning are given?	Meaning in your own words
1.			
2.			
3.			
4.			
5.			

Stepping Out, Reading and Viewing: Teacher's Resource 171

page 171

3 What am I looking for?

Observe whether students

- skim for particular words
- use context clues to guess meaning
- refer closely to the text to substantiate their interpretation
- demonstrate metacognition by:
  - explaining how to use context clues
  - applying the strategy independently

4 How can I collect information?

METHOD	EXAMPLE
Self-assessment Peer assessment Teacher observations Data-driven decisions Criteria checklists Anecdotal information Parent input Portfolio	**Self-assessment** I learned from this activity how to read around a difficult word to find clues to the meaning of the word. **Criteria checklist**

Criteria checklist

CRITERIA	STUDENTS' NAMES			
Able to find particular words by skimming				
Knows how to find context clues				
Able to refer closely to the text to support his/her interpretation				

Reproducible Pages

CONTENTS

Marking Key for Interviewing

Topic: _____   Date: _____

Name of Interviewer: _____   Name of Interviewee: _____

A Content – 4 marks

1. Displays good evidence of research. ___

2. Constructs effective open-ended questions. ___

3. Questions display a good understanding of issues/topic. ___

4. Listens actively and constructs questions arising from comments made by interviewee. ___

B Manner – 4 marks

5. Confident manner. ___

6. Speaks clearly and audibly. ___

7. Gives appropriate body messages to interviewee. ___

8. Pace of delivery is appropriate. ___

C Method (Structure) – 2 marks

9. Interview contains a clear introduction. ___

10. Asks questions in a logical order. ___

TOTAL: ___

Adjudicator:

A Content – 4 marks

1. Displays good evidence of research. ___

2. Demonstrates a good understanding of topic/issues. ___

3. Supports ideas with appropriate examples and details. ___

4. Answers questions effectively. ___

B Manner – 4 marks

5. Answers questions confidently. ___

6. Speaks clearly and audibly. ___

7. Gives appropriate body messages to interviewee. ___

8. Pace of delivery is appropriate. ___

C Method (Structure) – 2 marks

9. Orders answers logically. ___

10. Keeps answers brief and addresses important ideas. ___

TOTAL: ___

■ Marking Key for Debating

Grade: _____

Class: _____

Topic: _____

Date: _____

	Affirmative			Negative		
	1st	2nd	3rd	1st	2nd	3rd
Names:						
	0 1 2	0 1 2	0 1 2	0 1 2	0 1 2	0 1 2

Content – 8 marks

1. The arguments used appeal to the average, reasonable person.

2. Displays a thorough understanding of the topic.

3. Develops arguments well and supports them with appropriate examples.

4. 1st speakers: Clearly define topic

    Other speakers: Refute opposition's arguments effectively

Manner – 8 marks

1. Speaker is clear and audible.

2. Maintains good eye contact with audience, keeps notes unobtrusive.

3. Effective pace of delivery

4. Confident and persuasive manner

Method – 4 marks

1. Speech was clearly organized into a beginning, a well-developed middle, and an end.

2. Made good use of time.

3. Showed evidence of the roles of different speakers (bonus mark).

Individual's Total (20)

Total Team Points (60)

■ Pros, Cons, and Questions

Issue: _____

_____

Pros	Cons

Questions: _____

_____

_____

_____

_____

_____

■ Rubric for Homework Questions

Name: _____ **Date:** _____

Content

20	18	16	14	12	10

- Clear understanding of material
- Ideas well supported by examples and explanations

- Good grasp of material
- Ideas supported by some examples and/or explanations

- Little understanding of material
- Little or no attempt to use supporting details or explanations

Mechanics

10	9	8	7	6	5

- Complete and accurate sentence structure
- Accurate spelling and grammar

- Minor errors in sentence structure and/or grammar
- Some proofreading or careless errors

- Incomplete sentences
- Numerous errors in spelling and/or grammar

Presentation

5	4	3	2

- Neatly written or typed
- Well organized
- On time

- Legible
- Good organization
- On time

- Difficult to read
- Poor organization
- Late

Work for Small Groups

Group Summarizing

Groups read and summarize each paragraph of an article or text by producing a single phrase that captures the essence of the paragraph. The phrases together should present a summary of the story. Students discuss whether the final result captures the meaning of the original article or text.

Discuss Part of a Textbook

Each group member reads a different section of a textbook. Students read silently then discuss what they read. Together the group arrives at a joint summary of the content. Monitor group discussions to determine common areas of difficulty which the whole class can discuss.

Picture Books

Groups create a picture book about a specific theme or concept.

Web Site

Groups create a school Web site.

Web Site Critique

Establish a framework of questions for students to use as they critique several Web sites. Sites can be pre-selected or left to students to select. Students should focus on the source of the Web site, the target audience, the assumptions it makes, the type of language used, any claims made, and so on.

Use Presentation Software

Students develop a ten-minute promotional presentation about a topic of their choice, using presentation software. Students might use interviewing skills, role-play, music, digital images, sound effects, cartoons, and so on. Negotiate a marking key and have students submit drafts as part of the final assessment.

Book Review

Groups present a multimedia book review to the class. Presentations might include biographical information, career details, historical context, sample text, a critique of the work, and so on.

Multi-Media Projects

Students critique a range of references, for example print, television, encyclopedia, Internet, about the same topic. They can use focus questions to guide their reading/viewing, including those that help students identify the attitudes and beliefs conveyed in the texts.

■ SWOT Analysis

Strengths What are the strengths of the text?	**Weaknesses** What are the limitations of the text?
Opportunities What are other potential applications?	**Threats** What risks are involved?

■ Sentence Starters for Developing Questions

These sentence starters can help you develop questions.

1. Knowledge
- List the steps for . . .
- Identify the characteristics of . . .
- Define the term . . .
- Restate the events that led to . . .

2. Understanding
- In your own words, what happened to . . .
- Put these concepts in order . . .
- Give examples of . . .
- Why did . . . ?

3. Application
- Put the ideas on a chart or diagram.
- Draw a map to show . . .
- Calculate the . . .
- Retell this story from the point of view of . . .

4. Analysis
- If this happens, then . . . ?
- What is the relationship between . . . and . . . ?
- What is the difference between the concept . . . and the fact that . . . ?
- What are the most significant developments . . . ?

5. Synthesis
- Create a new plan that . . .
- Write a new ending so that . . .
- Put yourself in the situation. What would you have done?
- What would have happened if . . . ?

6. Evaluation
- Tell why you think that . . .
- To what extent did . . .
- Rate the options that . . .
- In your opinion . . .

■ Previewing a Text

Predict	• Read the front cover and back blurb. • Based on your reading, predict what the textbook will be about. • Make a list of questions that you think the book will answer. • Look at the write-up about the author: What do you think are the qualifications for writing a book like this? What does the author have to know?
Identify Publishing Information	Locate the publishing information: • When was the book published? • In your opinion, does this make it a "recent" publication? • How many reprints have there been? • Why do you think that a publisher would reprint a book? What does that tell you about the content? about the author?
Explore the Textbook Structure	• Skim/scan the contents page. • How many chapters are there? Check out two or three chapters: • How are the chapters laid out? • Are all the chapters laid out the same way? • Are there chapter summaries, study guides, questions, pictures, maps, charts? • Is there a glossary or index? • Is there a reference list? • Are there notes at the back of the book? What are they about?
Share Predictions	With a partner, compare your observations on the textbook so far: • What topic or topics does the book cover? • What do you think that you'll be expected to learn from this text? • How do you see yourself using this book? • How easy or hard does it appear to be? • Can you find specific information in this book easily? • What predictions can you make about this book? How will you use it? How will your teacher use it? How would you *like* it to be used?

(continued)

▪ Previewing a Text (continued)

Understand the Chapter Layout	Select a chapter: • Is the chapter well set out? • Are there clear headings? • Are there subheadings? How do the subheadings add to your understanding of what the chapter is about? • Read a paragraph: Are there unfamiliar words? Are the words explained? Are you going to have to use a dictionary to understand some of the terms? Does the book refer you to the glossary to explain words? • Are there illustrations? Are there clear captions with the illustrations to explain the content? • What other characteristics of this chapter did you notice?
Identify the Reading Level of the Textbook	• Is the print in this book easy to read? • Are the words easy to follow and understand? • Are there many difficult words on the page? • Try the "five-finger exercise": Start reading at the top of a page. Each time that you read a word that you don't understand, hold up one finger. If you hold up five fingers by the end of the page, you may find the book challenging. • Are new words introduced, highlighted or explained?
Quick Quiz	• Locate a chapter in this book on [choose a topic]. • Where was the book published? • Where will you find this word [insert word] explained in the book?

Generate Questions	• With a partner, make a list of five or six questions about the book that will be of interest to you and your classmates. Think about:
	
	  – how the book might be used
	
	  – where you will find information on a particular topic
	
	  – what other resources you might have to use to supplement the textbook
	
	  – what films, TV shows, books, or magazines you know that connect to the topics in this textbook

Independent Task	• With other pairs, share your questions and try to answer them. • Share unanswered questions with the whole class for resolution.

■ Note-making Framework

Topic: _____

Text title: _____

First paragraph

Main idea:

Examples, supporting ideas, key words:

1.

2.

3.

Second paragraph

Main idea:

Examples, supporting ideas, key words:

1.

2.

3.

Scavenger Hunt Question Outline

Prediction

- Read the front cover and back blurb. Identify the clues about the textbook's subject.

- Make a list of five questions that you think the book will answer.

- What do you think are the author's qualifications for writing a book like this? What does the author have to know?

Introduction

- Locate the publishing information and find out when the book was published.

- How many reprints have there been?

- Why do you think that a publisher would reprint a book? What does that tell you about the content? the author?

- In your opinion, does this make it a "recent" publication? Why?

Overview of the Book's Structure

- How many chapters are there?

- Check out two or three chapters: How are the chapters laid out? Are all the chapters laid out the same way? Are there chapter summaries, study guides, questions, pictures, maps, charts?

- Is there a glossary or index?

- Is there a reference list?

- Are there notes at the back of the book? Briefly tell what they are about.

Sharing Predictions

- With your partner, compare your observations on the textbook so far:

- What topic does the book cover?

- What do you think that you'll be expected to learn from this text?

- How do you see yourself using this book?

- How easy or hard does it appear to be?

- Can you find specific information in this book easily?

- What predictions can you make about this book: How will you use it? How will the teacher use it? How would you like it to be used?

(continued)

■ Scavenger Hunt Question Outline (continued)

Individual Chapter Layout

• Select a chapter.

• Are there headings in the chapter?

• Are there subheadings? How do the subheadings add to your understanding of what the chapter is about?

• Select one paragraph. Read it. Are there unfamiliar words? Are the words explained? Are you going to have to use a dictionary to understand some of the terms? Is there a glossary in the book to explain the words?

• Are there illustrations in this chapter? Are there clear captions with the illustrations to explain the content?

• List three other characteristics of this chapter.

Terminology

• On a scale of 1 to 5 where 5 is the highest, rate the print in this book: Is it easy to read?

• Using the same 1 to 5 scale, rate the words in the text: Are they easy to follow and understand?

• Are there many difficult words on the page?

• Try the "five-finger exercise": Start reading at the top of a page. Each time that you read a word that you don't understand, hold up one finger. If you hold up five fingers by the end of the page, then the book may be challenging for you. Give the results of your five-finger exercise.

• Are new words introduced, highlighted, or explained?

Questions

• With a partner, make a list of five questions about the book that will be of interest to you and your classmates. Think about:
  – how the book might be used
  – where you will find information on a particular topic
  – what other resources you might have to use to supplement the textbook
  – what films, TV shows, books, or magazines you know that connect to the topics in this textbook

■ Summary Sheet

Topic/Heading: _____

Note-making	Summarizing	
Sub-headings	**Key words and phrases**	**In my own words— subheadings and paragraphs**

■ Think-Aloud Comments

Visualizing

"What I see is . . ."

"I imagine that this looks like . . ."

Monitoring comprehension

"I'm having trouble understanding how . . ."

"I'm finding this difficult because . . ."

"I think I'm going to have to re-read this paragraph to understand it."

"To make sure I've got this, I'm going to over the points again."

Clarifying

"Maybe I should stop and look up this word."

"I have this question about what I just read."

Comparing

"I can compare what's happening now to what we learned earlier."

"This part reminds me of . . ."

Predicting

"I bet that . . ."

"I think what's going to happen next is . . ."

Connecting

"The connection between what I've just read and science/drama/history/TV/ yesterday's story is . . ."

Commenting

"If you think about it, this part is . . ."

"I think the author is doing a good job because . . ."

Questioning the text

"I wonder what the writer means by this sentence."

"I thought that we learned that . . ."

■ Think Sheet

Question 1

Prediction

Supporting detail from the text (page number _____)

Question 2

Prediction

Substantiation (page number _____)

Question 3

Prediction

Substantiation (page number _____)

■ Three Levels of Questions

On the page Literal	Between the lines Inferential	Off the page Evaluative
What countries are represented in this map? What factors cause stress? What patterns are reflected in the table? What is globalization? List the six major branches of psychology. What is body language? What is an improper fraction? When and where was Dylan Thomas born? What is a rhetorical question? How do savings bonds help an individual to plan for and save money?	What makes an effective leader? Why do so many people have a difficult time controlling their intake of substances such as alcohol, tobacco, and other drugs? How do you know that 2.3 is greater than 2.27? Create a visual representation (such as a collage, collection of objects, or a sketch) that conveys the overall mood and theme of this story. What happens if a person plans a budget based on the gross income listed on his or her pay slip?	Why is it important in a society such as ours that education institutions should recognize and reward merit in many different forms? Thin is in. Explain whether you agree or disagree with this statement. Write a fraction or a mixed number to make this statement true: $1\frac{3}{7} < \frac{\square}{\square} < 2\frac{1}{7}$ In what ways does this story follow the archetypal pattern of quest myths? What is the potential for bartering in the future? What would you recommend to a person who has a difficult time saving any money but wishes to invest? Why?

Vocabulary in Context

Read around difficult words in order to infer meaning.

Word/phrase	Page number	What clues to meaning are given?	Meaning in your own words
1.			
2.			
3.			
4.			
5.			

References and Acknowledgements

This list credits all references cited and all copyrighted material reprinted. Every effort has been made to find and acknowledge the copyright holder. Should you have further information about copyrighted material, please contact the publisher.

Alberta Learning, Social Studies 10-20-30, 2001.

Anthony, R., Johnson, T., Mickelson, N., Preece, A. (1991), Evaluating Literacy- a Perspective for Change, Rigby Heinemann, Australia.

Education Department of Western Australia (1999), Focusing on outcomes: Curriculum, Assessment and Reporting, Case Study 12, p 85.

Barber, M. (1999), Taking the Tide at the Flood of Transforming Education in the Middle Years, (Plenary Address, The Middle Years of Schooling Conference, Melbourne).

Barrett, R. (1998), Point and Counterpoint. The Future: The Shape of Middle Schooling in Australia. Curriculum Perspectives, p 18 (1).

Barrie, R. et al. (Eds.) (2000), *Advocating Change: Contemporary Issues in Subject English*, Irwin Publishers.

Berkley, G. (1994), Middle Years of Schooling – A School Council Perspective, *Unicorn*, 20 (2), pp 5-11.

Beane, James, (1990), A Middle School Curriculum from Rhetoric to Reality, NMSA p.49.

Beane, J. (1991), The Middle School: The Natural Home of the Integrated Curriculum, *Educational Leadership*, October 1991. 49 (2), pp9-13.

Beane, J. (1993), The Search for a Middle School Curriculum *The School Administrator*, 50 (3), pp 8-14.

Beane, J. (1995), Curriculum Integration and the Disciplines of Knowledge, *Phi Delta Kappan*, April, 1995. Pp 616-622.

Beane, J. and Brodhagen (B.) (1995), Negotiating an Integrated Curriculum Unit of Study. *What Does the Middle School Curriculum Look Like?* The Middle Years Kit. Videoconference at the ATC/NSN Middle Years Development School, Adelaide, April, 1995.

Beers, Kylene (2003), *When Kids Can't Read: What Teachers Can Do*, Heinemann, Portsmouth, NH.

Bennett, Barrie, and Carol Rolheiser (2001), *Beyond Monet: The Artful Science of Instructional Integration*, Bookation, Inc., Toronto.

Berkley, G. (1994), Middle Years of Schooling – A Schools Council Perspective. *Unicorn*, 20 (2), pp 5-11.

Bigum, C. & Green, B (1993a), Aliens in the Classroom, *Australian Journal of Education*. 37 (2), pp 119-141.

Bigum, C. & Green, B. (1993b), Technologising literacy; or, interrupting the dream of reason. In P. Gilbert & A. Luke (Eds) Literacy in Contexts: Australian perspectives and Issues, 4-28. Sydney: Allen & Unwin.

Brandes, D., Ginnis, P. and Hammond L. (1990), *The Student Centred School: Ideas for Practical Visionaries,* Oxford Blackwell Education, p 13.

Brennan, M. & Sachs, J. (1998), *Curriculum, Classroom Materials for the Middle Years,* Australian Curriculum Studies Association, Canberra.

Bruner, J. (1986), *Actual Minds, Possible Worlds,* Cambridge University Press, London.

Cairney, T.H. (1992), Literacy for All: Exploding the Myths of Literacy, *International Conference Committee,* Australian Reading Association, Carlton, Victoria.

Cairney, T.H. and Ruge, J. (1996), Examining the Impact of Cultural Mismatches Between Home and School: Coping with Diversity in Classrooms, Paper presented to American Association for Educational Research Conference, New York.

Cairney, T.H. and Ruge, J. (1997), Community Literacy Practices and Schooling – Towards Effective Support for Students, Executive Summary, Department of Employment, Education, Training and Youth Affairs.

Cairney, T.H., Lowe K. and Sproats, E. (1995), *Literacy in Transition: An Investigation of the Literacy Practices of Upper Primary and Junior Secondary Schools,* (Vol 1-3), D.E.E.T., Canberra.

Chapman, A. (1996), Current Trends in Language, Literacy and Classroom Mathematics. Literacy and Learning in Mathematics. Curriculum Support in Mathematics. *Stepping Out.* Education Department of Western Australia.

Clarke, J., Wideman, R., and Eadie, S. (1990), *Together We Learn – Co-Operative Small Group Learning,* Prentice-Hall, Canada. Inc. Scarborough, Ontario.

Comber, B. (1998), Literacies, Contingent Repertoires and School Success, Garth Boomer Memorial Address, Joint National Conference of Australian ALEA and the ETA, Canberra.

Cumming, J. (1994a), Educating Young Adolescents – an ASCA discussion paper, *Curriculum Perspectives,* Newsletter edition, November, pp 36-39.

Cumming, J. (1994b), Catering For the Needs of all Young Adolescents; Towards an Integrated Approach. *Unicorn,* 20 (2), pp 12-20.

Cumming, J. (1996), *From Alienation to Engagement: Opportunities for Reform in the Middle Years of Schooling* (Vol 3), Australian Curriculum Studies Association, Belconnen, ACT.

Cumming, J. (1999), Into the Community. An edited extract published in Education Quarterly, Issue Four, Summer 1999. Curriculum Corporation, Melbourne, from *The Guide to Effective Community Based Learning.* Australian College of Education, PO Box 323, Deakin West, ACT 2600.

Cumming, J. Wyatt-Smith, C. Ryan, J. and Doig, S. (1998), *The Literacy-Curriculum Interface. The Literacy Demands of the Curriculum in Post-compulsory Schooling,* Executive Summary, Department of Employment, Education, Training and Youth Affairs. Griffith University, ACT.

Curriculum Corporation, Carlton Victoria. Oodles of Noodles; Integrated Units Collection.

Daniels, Harvey (1994), *Literature Circles: Voice and Choice in the Student-Centered Classroom*, Stenhouse Publishers.

Daniels, Harvey and Bizar, Marilyn (1998), *Methods That Matter*, Stenhouse Publishers.

Daniels, Harvey and Steineke, Nancy (2004), *Mini-Lessons for Literature Circles*, Heinemann.

Daniels, Harvey and Zemelman, Steven (2004), *Subjects Matter*, Heinemann.

Darling-Hammond, Linda and Loewenber Ball, Deboarah (1997), "Teaching for High Standards: What Policymakers Need to Know and Be Able to Do." Paper prepared for the National Educational Goals Panel, June 1997. (United States)

Dimmock, C. (1993), University of Western Australia. Cited in Benda, D. (1993). Flexibility is the Key. *West Australian* Newspaper. Date of publication not known.

Earl, L. and Hargreaves, A. (1990), *Rights of Passage: A Review of Selected Research about Schools in the Transition Years*, Ontario Ministry for Education, Toronto.

Elmore, Richard (2002), *Bridging the Gap Between Standards and Achievement: The Imperative for Professional Development in Education*, Albert Shanker Institute (www.shankerinstitute.org).

Eyers, V. (1993), Educating Young Adolescents. In J. Cumming and D. Flemming (Eds), *In the Middle or at the Centre? A Report on a National Conference on Middle Schooling*, Australian Curriculum Studies Association, Belconnen, ACT.

Eyers, V. et al. (1992), *The Education of Young Adolescents in South Australian Government Schools*. Report of the Junior School Review, Adelaide Education Department, South Australia.

Fedlaufer, H. Midgley, C. and Eccles, J. (1998), Students, teacher and observer perceptions of the classroom environment before and after the transition to junior high school, *Journal of Early Adolescence*, pp 133-156.

Fullan, M. and Hargreaves, A. (1991), *Working Together for your School*. Australian Council for Education Administration, Inc., Paperbacks, Victoria, Australia pp 52-53.

Galton, M., Gray, J. and Rudduck, J. (1999), *The Impact of School Transitions and Transfers on Student Progress and Attainment*, DEE, London.

Gee, J. (1990), *Social Linguistics and Literacies: Ideology in Discourses*, Falmer Press, London.

Gill, M. (1998), Who Set the Benchmarks? Analysing the National Literacy Agenda. *English in Australia*. 121.

Ginsburg, H. (1989), *Children's Arithmetic: How They Learn it and How You Teach It*, Pro. Ed., Austin.

Glasser, W (1993), *The Quality School Teacher*, Harper Collins, New York.

Golub, Jeffrey N. (2000), *Making Learning Happen*, Heinemann.

Goodman, Y. (1985), Kid Watching: Observing Children in the Classroom. In A. Jagger and M. Smith-Bourke's *Observing the Language Learner*, Newark, DE: International Reading Association.

Government of British Columbia Ministry of Education, Mathematics Curriculum, 2001.

Green, B. and Bigum, C. (1993), Aliens in the Classroom, *Australian Journal of Education*, 37 (2), pp 119-141.

Halliday, M.A.K. (1973), *Explorations in the Functions of Language*, Arnold, London.

Hardy, J. and Klarwein, D. (1990), *Written Genres in the Secondary School*, Department of Education, Queensland.

Hargreaves, A. (1998), Middle Schooling "Communicate clear messages," *The West Australian*, Monday, October 19, 1998. (Reporter: K Ashworth).

Hargreaves, Andy; Earl, Lorna; Moore, Shawn; and Manning, Susan (2001), *Learning to Change: Teaching Beyond Subjects and Standards*, Jossey-Bass Inc., San Francisco.

Hill, P. (1993), *School and Teacher Effectiveness in Victoria: Key Findings of the Victorian Quality Schools Project*, University of Melbourne, Melbourne.

Hill, P. and Crevola, C. (1999), Characteristics of an Effective Literacy Strategy, *Unicorn*, 24, 2, August.

Kenworthy, C. & Kenworthy, S. (1997*), Changing Places – Aboriginality in Texts and Contexts*, Fremantle Arts Press, Western Australia.

Kiddey, P. (2000), So What's Different About Learning in the Middle and Secondary School Context? *Journal of the Australian Literacy Educators' Association*, Volume 8, Number 1, Melbourne, Victoria.

Kirkpatrick, D. (1995), The Transition from Primary to Secondary School: Self Regulated Learning and Achievement Motivation, PhD thesis, Edith Cowan University, Western Australia.

Kress, G. (1985), *Linguistic Processes in Sociocultural Practice*, Deakin University, Victoria.

Kress, G. (1996), New London Group. A Pedagogy of Multiliteracies. Designing Social Futures, *Harvard Educational Review*, 66 (1) pp 60-91.

Kress, G. (1999) cited in Wyatt-Smith, C & Cumming, J., Examining the Literacy Demands of the Enacted Curriculum, *Literacy Learning: Secondary Thoughts, 7, 2.*

Leithwood, Ken and McAdie, Pat (2005), "Less is more: the Ontario Curriculum that we need," *Orbit*, Vol. 35, no. 1.

Lemke, J. (1999), cited in Wyatt-Smith, C. & Cumming, J., Examining the Literacy Demands of the Enacted Curriculum, *Literacy Learning: Secondary Thoughts, 7, 2.*

Lountain, K. & Dumbleton, M. (1999), On Home Territory, *Education Quarterly*, Issue 4, Summer, 1999, Curriculum Corporation, Victoria.

Lountain, K. & Dumbleton, M. (1999), Unlocking Literacy, *Education Quarterly*, Issue 4, Summer 1999, Curriculum Corporation, Victoria.

Luke, A. (1995). Multimedia: Multiliteracies. *Education Australia*. Issue 30, 1995. James Cook University, Queensland.

Martin, J.R. (1985), Factual Writing: Exploring and Challenging Social Reality.

Masters, G. & Forster, M. (1996), Developmental Assessment Resource Kit, Australian Council of Educational Research, Victoria, Australia.

Mathematics and Natural Sciences Branch, Curriculum and Instruction Division, Saskatchewan Education (1991), Science K-12 Curriculum.

Morgan, P. (1993), The Time Has Come, *National Schools (Australia) Network Issues Paper*, No. 1.

Morris, A. and Stewart Dore, N. (1984), *Learning to Learn from Text: Effective Reading in the Content Areas*, Addison-Wesley, NSW.

Murphy, C. (1997) Finding Time for Faculties to Study Together. Journal of Staff Development, Summer, 1997.

National Council of Teachers of English (2004), *A Call to Action: What We Know About Adolescent Literacy and Ways to Support Teachers in Meeting Students' Needs.*

New London Group (1996), A Pedagogy of Multiliteracies. Designing Social Futures. *Harvard Educational Review*, 66 (1) pp 60-91.

NSW Department of School Education (1997), Literacy 97 Strategy, Focus on Literacy.

Ontario College of Teachers (1999), *Standards of Practice for the Teaching Profession.*

The Ontario Curriculum, Grades 9 and 10: The Arts, 1999.

Pirie, Bruce (2002), *Teenage Boys and High School English*, Heinemann.

Pressley, M. (2000), Comprehensive Instruction in Elementary School: A Quarter Century of Research Progress in Reading for Meaning; Fostering Comprehension in the Middle Grades. Teachers College Press. IRA Newark. DE19714.

Project of National Significance (1996), National MSA Newsletter Australian Curriculum Studies Association.

Reid, J., Forrestal, P. Cook, J. (1989), *Small Group Learning in the Classroom*, Primary English Association – Chalkface Press, Western Australia.

Rosenholtz, S. (1989), *Teachers' Workplace: The Social Organisation of Schools*, New York: Longman.

Rosenthal, R. and Jacobsen, L. (1968), *Pygmalion in the Classroom; Teacher Expectation and Students' Intellectual Development*, Holt, Rhinehart and Winston, New York.

Rudduck, J., Chaplain, R., and Wallace, C. (1996), *School Improvement: What Can Students Tell Us?* Fulton, London.

SA Field Study (1994), as reported in *Curriculum Perspectives*, 15, 2, June 1995, Australian Curriculum Studies Association.

Sawyer, W. (1999), Testing the Benchmarks, Literacy and Year 7, *English in Australia*, 124.

Schools Council Report (*State Board of Education*, Victoria, 1990 p 24) (in *Schools Council* document p 87).

Snyder, I. (1996), Integrating Computers into the Literacy Curriculum: More Difficult Than We First Imagined, *Australian Journal of Language and Literacy*, 19,4, pp 330-344.

Smith, Michael and Wilhelm, Jeffrey D. (2002), *"Reading Don't Fix No Chevys": Literacy in the Lives of Young Men*, Portsmouth.

Stenmark, J. (1991), Mathematics Assessment: Myths, Models, Good Questions, and Practical Suggestions. National Council of Teachers of Mathematics. Virginia, USA.

Strickland, Kathleen and James (1998), *Reflections on Assessment*, Boynton/Cook, Portsmouth, New Hampshire.

South Australian Film Corporation, *Lingo Video*, Film and Video distribution, 3 Butler Drive, Westside Commercial Centre, Tapleys Hill Road, Heydon, South Australia, 5014.

Spender, Dale (1995), *Nattering on the Net. Women, Power and Cyberspace*, Spinifex Press North Melbourne.

Students, SA Field Study, 1994, Project of National Significance (1996) National Middle School Association Newsletter.

Ungerleider, Charles (2005), "The Challenge of Secondary Curriculum Reform," *Orbit* Magazine, vol. 35, No. 1.

Vygotsky, L.S. (1966), *Thought and Language* (A. Kozulin, Trans) MIT Press, Cambridge, MA.

Vygotsky, L.S. (1978), *Mind in Society: The Development of Higher Mental Psychological Processes*, Harvard University Press, Cambridge, MA.

Vygotsky, L.S. (1978), *Mind in Society*. MIT Press, Cambridge, MA.

Vygotsky, L.S. (1986), *Thought and Language* (New Edition), Harvard University Press, Cambridge, MA.

Warhurst, J (1994), Understanding Cross Curricular Practice in Schools. ACSA Occasional Paper, No 5, Dec. 1994.

Westwood, P. (1995), Teachers' Beliefs and Expectations Concerning Students with Learning Difficulties. In *Australian Journal of Remedial Education*, 27, 2, pp 19-21.

Wilson, B. (1999), Schooling: What Matters? *Education Quarterly*, Curriculum Corporation, Melbourne, Summer 1999, Editorial, p 3.

Wilson, J. and Wing Jan, L. (1993), *Thinking for Themselves, Developing Strategies for Reflective Learning*. Eleanor Curtain Publishing, Armadale. Victoria.

Wyatt-Smith, C. & Cumming, J. (1999), Examining the Literacy Demands of the Enacted Curriculum. *Literacy Learning: Secondary Thoughts* 7, 2.

Index

transfer, elementary-secondary 4
transportable tools 10
tutor models 58

V

visual literacy 52
Vocabulary in Context Strategy 152-53

W

whole-class learning 27
withdrawal of students 56
Web 31
writing, guided 37